The Goldfisl

Seven Actions to Distinguish Yourself for Success

Jack W. Peters

Editor

Joan Raymond
JoanRaymondWriting.com

jack@donorthmedia.com
www.donorthmedia.com
www.facebook.com/treasurequestjack/
PO Box 52, Walterville, Oregon 97489 USA

First Edition Release, November 2020

Amazon ISBN 9798563560260

Dedication

To my children, *Eric, Mikayla,* and *Mikenzie*. May you remember your roots and grow while finding your wings to soar!

Acknowledgements

Special thanks to those who helped make this book possible.

Editor

Joan Raymond, JoanRaymondWriting.com

Special thanks to:

Goldfish art designed by Tony McAlister, @reborn.ink
Reborn Ink Studio, Springfield, Oregon

Loyd 'Tom' Kruse, *Risky Business Desert Racing*,
who coined the phrase that became the title of this book.

Discovery Channel's *Treasure Quest* Bolivia, TV Series cast members: Jeremy Whalen, Shawn Cowles, and Javier Cortes, for allowing me to use their photos.

Rear cover photo by Sean Farr, Adak Island, Alaska,
During the filming of the Netflix Original Series, *Adak Gold*.

Other books in print by Jack W. Peters

Explosives and Blasting, 6th Edition

Explosives, IEDs and Breaching for Law Enforcement, 3rd Edition

Off the Grid Drive, Navigate & Survive Off-Road, 2nd Edition

Look for the *Rogue Captain* novel series beginning in 2021

CONTENTS

Chapter One
Start Right Now

I thought growing old would take longer. I remember when I turned 18 and graduated from high school, now I am 55. What happened? I lived an adventurous life of success, tragedy, love and loss with many blessings despite myself. And it is not over yet, in fact, I feel like things are just getting started. Older people say, "I wish I was young again, but knowing what I know now, I would rule the world." Well here is the ideal opportunity to learn some critical life wisdom from a guy who has been around the block a couple times.

This book is all about finding your strengths, discovering your passions, and then helping you determine what you can do to use your abilities to create the life you desire. This book is also about what you can do to distinguish yourself, giving you that edge to rise above the pack, and become discovered. Why is that important? Because as our world becomes smaller, the number of other people you will be competing against increases by the day. During our time together I will be asking you to ask honest questions of yourself. Like, what will your competitive edge be? And why would someone hire or promote you over someone else? If you are not sure how to answer, this book is for you.

Another question I will be asking is for you to take a hard, gut level look at your life's priorities and ambitions. If you are not sure, then it's all good, read on. If you do know, even better, but the next question is are you willing to do what it takes to reach your goals? You will see the primary theme of this book is you taking action. Planning and making decisions are important, but ultimately you taking action is most critical. The primary difference between successful people and unsuccessful people is successful people take action and learn from their experiences, then make adjustments and take more action!

I wish someone would have shared more of this information with me when I was younger. I might have been too stubborn to listen to it, but honestly, any solid advice would have helped. Life can have its share of heartache, frustration, and pain. Why experience any more of that than you must? Life is also full of joy, love, and opportunity. We need to focus on the positives if want to experience more of them. We were not put on the planet to just suffer through difficult times.

Having said that, it is the difficult times that try us, teach us, and help us to become stronger. Learn what you can learn, not only to survive this life, but also thrive. Exceed expectations so you can be a blessing to others. Helping others is where real happiness is found. But that starts with helping ourselves first. Create a foundation for successful life. In your professional and financial life, yes, but also in every aspect of your existence. Stronger relationships, learning, health, and exciting experiences as well as a meaningful spiritual connection.

Having this foundation will allow you to soar because you will be grounded in the fundamentals that provide the perfect launching pad to discover how high this life can take you. There are truly no limits on what you can do, but it is not easy or automatic. You must learn what you must, pay your dues, learn from others, and get out of your own way when the negative thoughts start telling you it is not possible. Others will do this and be wildly successful. You can too. Learn from them, learn from me, have confidence in yourself, and get started now.

Reverse Engineering

One year from this date you wake up and find your life just how you imagined it should be. You wake up next to the person you have dreamed about in a home you always wanted. If you want kids, yes, you kiss them on the forehead and tell them to have a great day. After breakfast you step into the garage and get into the car you have always wanted to drive. The combined smell of hot coffee and leather upholstery brings a smile to your face, you know it is going to be an amazing day.

You drive to work and step into the office. Your co-workers greet you with a smile and tell you how nice you look. No one needs to stand over you or tell you what to do. You dive into your tasks like a champion, kicking butt as the hours fly by. You check your bank account; it has a positive balance. You check the calendar and smile when you see the vacation days blocked out and look forward to some beach time with your love.

You are making progress, making money, helping others and having fun doing it. You are using your God-given talents and are on a mission. You feel you are doing exactly what you were meant to do. The combination of accomplishment, profit, and caffeine is euphoric. Life is not always perfect, but the momentum is going your way and you are feeling good!

Boom! Now it is time to snap back to today and ask yourself some important questions:

How did you get to that life?

_____

What specific steps did you need to take to get from here to there?

_____

What education did you need and how did you get it?

_____

Who did you need to meet to get your foot in the door?

_____

What toxic habits or people did you have to get rid of?

_____

What is holding you back from doing what you need to do to enjoy the life you want to have?

_____

This exercise is part of an effective improvement philosophy called *Appreciative Inquiry*. It discovers the value in asking and answering questions. Throughout this book I will be asking you to consider many important questions, and you will find that how you answer those questions will help guide you to meaningful and tangible improvements.

Green Light
I have used general platitudes in the introduction to help illuminate the big picture. To get there I am offering seven simple and specific actions you can do right now. Actions that do not require a great deal of money. What they do require is your time, commitment, and heart. I am not asking you to do anything I have not done. I had to discover and follow my own advice too. I promise you the effort will pay off.

You have broken the procrastination barrier, as the book is in your hands. There are no catches or anything else to buy so please read it with an open mind and open heart. Momentum is now moving in your direction and it will only become stronger as you advance toward a more positive and successful life. Nothing can stop you if you get out of your own way to get moving.

Chapter Two
Why Goldfish?

Jack winning an off-road desert race with driver, Loyd Kruse, the one who coined the phrase, "The Goldfish That Barked."

What's the Big Idea Anyway?

Success means different things to different people. Now is the time to ask what is your big idea? "What is your lifelong goal(s)? At what point do you consider yourself successful? If you don't have a large goal you would like to achieve, that's okay too. We will cover that topic in depth as we proceed.

Here are some examples of career goals:
Get accepted by your favorite college or university
Get hired by a dream employer
Own and operate your own company
Create a successful professional trade career
Create a successful sports career
Create a successful media career: author, actor, musician
Become a prestigious member of your professional community.
Become Five Mile Famous or know of internationally.

Having success in reaching these goals then helps you achieve many secondary goals that might include:

Financial Independence
Greater freedom with time and activities
Finding a compatible spouse
Getting married and raising children
Enjoying successful relationships with friends and family
Having the ability to help and support others
Enjoying an abundant and successful life
Having time and resources for bucket list items

These are just some examples of primary and secondary goals. You get the idea. The first goal is to get you the means, so you can accomplish the secondary goal of what you want to do in life. Here is your chance to strongly consider what you want to do in life. Don't just say I want a million dollars to buy a Ferrari. Be honest and specific. Maybe after further consideration, you really want to be a CPA and meet your soulmate? The questions are not as simple as they may seem, but it is it critical to know what you are playing for.

People ask, "How do you motivate someone?" Let them understand the consequences of winning and losing. What does it mean to win or be successful or what does it mean to lose or fail? Think carefully about what this means for you. Take the time to write these goals down. If you don't know what they are yet, come back to this exercise after you finish the book.

What are my primary goal(s): Career, Financial, what do you want to be known for?

_____

What are my secondary goal(s): Family, Home, Travel, Helping others?

_____

_____

What is it Worth to You?
Okay, now things are going to get serious. It is one thing to make life goals, but it is another thing to actually take action to see your plan through to success. Are you willing to do what it takes to maintain that million-dollar bank account and the Ferrari in the garage?

How about getting through college to obtain your CPA's license and then finding your soulmate?

If you say you want to be a professional athlete, you'd better be willing to get to the gym by 5 AM and work harder than anyone else to make the team. There are no shortcuts. Big dreams take big commitments. If you are not willing to do the work, then do not make the goals. By doing one and not the other, you are one of millions who want to lose weight, but never makes it to the gym. Then you tend to feel like a failure that disincentivizes you from making new goals in the future.

When you want something really bad, but your actions show that you do not, you have created *Cognitive Dissonance*. This is just a fancy way of saying you have internal conflict. You might hate the way you look naked in the mirror, but pizza and beer are just so delicious! You get the point. Life is all about decisions and determining what we will tolerate and what we will not. Time to be gut-wrenchingly honest and write down what you promise you are willing to do to reach your primary and secondary goals.

Keep in mind that you do not have to make goals or promise yourself what you will do to reach them. No one will care or force you to do this. Many drift through their entire life without doing any such thing. Just know that if you do not, fate will have its way with you and others will control your destiny.

Know that I am not telling you this because I am a master at discipline. Trust me, I am not. I can waste time like a pro. I get frustrated with myself for extensive procrastination at times, requiring a tough talk to get myself back on track. That is why I am sharing this with you.

What will I promise to do to reach my goals?

_____

Barking Goldfish?
The Goldfish That Barked is all about small simple, achievable improvements in your life that will add up to big positive changes. They will also help you distinguish yourself to stand out among the millions of others who pretty much want to do, or are already doing, what you want to do. (Hence the barking goldfish).

The phrase was coined by my desert off-road racing friend, Loyd Kruse.

We are were at a desert race and having around a campfire after the best day ever and Loyd was telling us about a shopping mall complex he bought. We looked at him in amazement. How did you do that?! He told us the story about how he worked and save to own rental properties, then traded them for the shopping center, "I was the goldfish that barked!"

I really like that idea of finding was and working hard to stand out, to distinguish yourself. Being successful, having fun, giving back, being the goldfish that barked!

Why Listen to Me?

I know what you are thinking. An adventure guy on TV, Jack looks like a friend of my dad's. I am probably old enough to be your dad (for many of you) and I am still having a pretty amazing and somewhat charmed life.

Way back before graduating from high school, my career guidance counselor looked and me, then looked at my grades and said, "Have you ever considered a career in small engine repair?" It is not that I disliked school, I just did not understand the connection between what I was learning and where I was going.

And at 18, who knows where they are going? Some are lucky enough to have direction, even pick out a major as they prepare for college. Life is unpredictable, even if you have a plan. Believe me, it can change fast as the economy, political events, and technological advances fluctuate like the weather. I had to grow up, focus, learn, adapt, and survive in an unpredictable world. You will too.

I put myself through college, got an internship, mentors, learned new careers, and rolled with the punches. I enjoy speaking, training, and writing books. I own and manage a media company and a specialty blasting company that does explosives training and specialty jobs.

I am one of four guys and the explosives specialist on *Discovery Channel's Treasure Quest* TV series. The last series we filmed in the mountains of Bolivia, South America, looking for two billion dollars' worth of lost Jesuit treasure. I am also the blaster on *Netflix's Series, Adak Gold*, where I detonate a WWII shell on Adak Island, Alaska.

Why am I so passionate about sharing these ideas with you? Well, because I wish someone would have told me.

I acquired the scares from learning the hard way. Years of wasted time and money, failed relationships and hard lessons learned.

In this book, I ask you to find your superpower and your life's mission. Mine appears to be the ability to organize ideas so others can easily learn from them. One of my life's missions is to share this book with as many people as possible from around the world. If you find a benefit in what you will read, please help me with sharing this information also.

Back to Basics

Simple is good. It is understandable and doable. That is the idea behind this book. I am not going to try to baffle you or look important with mystery formulas, gimmicks, or complex secrets only a PhD can understand. In fact, the ideas I provide in this book are so simple, anyone can understand them. Yet so effective, you will hopefully want to implement them right now.

Throughout this book, you will see I continue to cover some basic themes. This includes: Do not give yourself any self-inflicted handicaps or speedbumps along the way. Second is to learn from others so you accelerate instead of wasting time repeating mistakes. Another is to discover your superpower to give you an edge in pursing your life's mission. Here is the seven action topics we will cover in detail:

7.   **Build you Brand**

6.   **Do Not Fall Into Traps**

5.   **Learn to Communicate**

4.   **Educate Yourself**

3.   **Find Your Superpower**

2.   **Give Thanks**

1.   **Find Your Mission**

Thank you in advance for taking this journey with me. Be prepared to have your life immediately changed for the better! Okay, enough bloviating. Let's get down to business.

Chapter Three

Action 7. Building Your Brand

Disney is a master at branding. What can we learn from them?

When we think about brands, they could be positive, neutral, or negative. It seems we feel strongly about a brand in a positive or negative way. We want to share the brand and spend money on it or avoid it at all costs. This works out great for the brand when others want to wear their t-shirt, tell their friends and spending money on it. Of course, this publicity cuts the other way too. If the brand is not good, we are happy to share that news too. One or two bad reviews can kill sales.

When we think about brands there are lots to choose from. Including companies, cars, movies, clothing, virtually everything has a brand. Even perfume and sports teams are carefully branded. But, what about people? Of course, politicians, CEOs, actors, musicians, authors, and all types of celebrities have their own brand. That means you, and what you produce are a brand too. No pressure, but everything you do, say, post and how you look effects your brand in a positive or negative way. In a social media for example, when you hit send on a post, do others want to like and share it or unfriend you?

Don't Judge a Book by its Cover?
How else do you expect someone to judge you?

You judged this book by its cover, hopefully enough that it inspired you to buy and read it. Truth is, within seconds we size up people every day by the way they appear. It is just human nature. Within a moment we know if we would be willing to talk to them, do business with them, be friends with them, even fall in love with them. Or, maybe avoid them all together. This is all how we subconsciously perceive others based upon what brand they are projecting. In the simplest terms from centuries of human survival, we get a gut level impression if a new person will be a benefit or a determent. Surprisingly, this gut level reaction can be quite accurate.

I know this is somewhat superficial, and maybe not fair, but it is human nature. We are typically much more than just our appearance, but the goal is getting successfully through the initial appearance and impression. We often get the wrong impression of someone either in a positive or negative way, but it takes extra mental work to change our mind once we have confirmed a first impression. That guy who looks and acts like a dirty bum might be a great guy, but it might take too much mental energy to get past the dirty bum part. What is interesting is that through experiences and time, your opinion can change now that you know he is indeed a good person, but you brain still defaults to – dirty bum.

Understand you are your own brand. Those you meet, (like it or not) will size you up in a first impression within moments. Their impression will either be reinforced or eventually changed over time based upon your ongoing actions or performance. Every action, look and image, in person and online should reflect your brand in the greatest light possible.

Look at your favorite brands and learn from them. Maybe a rock band or an athlete, a beverage, a clothing line, or maybe a well-known company. Look that their name, logo, images, website, and messaging. Everything you see and read is typically very consistent and polished. Public relations specialists work hard to project a certain and specific look and image. This is what helps sell their client's products.

All these many aspects of you and your business are like chapters in a book. The sum of your overall appearance is the cover. I am asking you to be your own public relations specialist. Look closely at your brand. What is working for you now and how do you make it even better?

Remember the adage about you only get one chance to make the best first impression? This is true. Do not attempt to sell your brand until you are ready to shine. Be patient, it's worth it to do it right the first time.

Do You Look Like a Million Bucks?

Would you believe that is what an employer could spend on you? By the time they recruit and train you, then pay your salary with benefits over the years. Depending how high profile the job is, that million-dollar mark could come very quickly. Regardless of how long it might take, most employers or clients see their next key person as a long-term investment. They will invest considerable time and money into them hoping for a win-win mutually beneficial relationship lasting possibly decades.

Are you ready for someone to make an investment in you now? This sounds simple, but if your dream employer called you for an interview this week to start on Monday, would you be ready? It is been said that success is when an opportunity meets one who is prepared to take advantage of it. Isn't that the truth? Being ready for success means improving and updating your brand on an ongoing basis.

Leveraging a Paperclip into a Ferrari

So, what if you are young, just starting out, have nothing, and no one knows you. That is perfectly okay. We have all been there and we all must start somewhere. Some of the largest companies you can think of started with so little it would make you laugh.

All the big computer and software companies like *Amazon, Apple, Google* and *Microsoft* started in a garage. The shoe giant *Nike* got their start by making running shoe soles with a waffle iron. Sir Richard Branson of the *Virgin* empire started by selling Christmas trees and parakeets. Steve Wynn of *Wynn Resorts* is credited for revitalizing Las Vegas started by inheriting bingo parlors $300,000 in debt. *Facebook* started in a Harvard dorm room. The founders of *Mattel* toys started making doll house furniture out of picture frame scraps. The mega media empire of *Disney* all began with Walt's drawing of a mouse in a small Los Angeles apartment.

There are thousands of examples of successful companies starting with practically nothing. The fact is successful people and companies do not start big at all.

It is someone who has an idea who then turns it into a dream to see the idea through. Eventually the idea turns into a product or service which becomes a brand. But this does not happen overnight. Overnight successes typically have 20 years of hard work behind them. All the founders in the above examples worked their butts off every day. They did not give up, they kept working and recruiting others to help them until they had something tangible. Something others could buy into to help the dream grow.

These founders also did not rely solely on looks and image. They had to provide a product and service to back up any image they projected. There is no shortcut for this. Building a successful career company and brand can take years. Hard work every day. Getting better every day. Always looking for new ideas, innovation, and technology. Always looking for the right people who share the dream and want to help fulfill the mission.

Small improvements, victories and advances every day, every week, every year until all the hard work pays off in a big win. Being successful is not a get-rich-quick scheme. It is a long-term investment starting with you. Even if the only thing you have to offer is a smile, a positive attitude, and a handshake, just get started.

What If They Want to Contact You?

Let us start with the very basics. Your future employer or client is trying to contact you right now. What does your outgoing message sound like on your cell phone? If I get a computer-generated message with no name, I wonder who they are hiding from and usually hang up. Or worse, the message that the mailbox is full and cannot take new messages. How about your email address? What does it look like? If you have goofy email address, you will not be taken seriously, especially if your message gets deleted before it can be opened and read. Email addresses are free, get a good one, or better yet, pay $5 a month and get a custom professional one.

Going Social

Know where I am going next? That's right, social media. Anyone that is going to hire you or give you that once in a lifetime opportunity is going to look at your social media. They will, trust me. You can say its private and your business only, but what you post and comment on is largely in the public domain forever. Why does this matter?

Before they invest large amounts of money and time into you, they want to know who you really are.

They can see what you look like during a job interview, but social medial lets someone see what you look like in your personal life. You might be able to behave yourself and look professional on a business site like *LinkedIn*, but the real you could be after a few drinks tagged in a post on *Facebook* or *Instagram*. Even if you block your page from non-friends, you would be surprised to see what someone can still get on you.

It is a great idea to go through your media pages and delete anything that looks questionable. People can tag you in photos that you long forgot about that may not show you the best light. If you cannot get them to delete them, at least un-tag yourself. No one wants to hear you continually complain. You might garnish some very temporary sympathy, but ultimately you are turning people off. Another turn off is crude language. Yes, you can cuss online, so can everyone else and it is not impressive. In fact, it makes you look low class.

Use social media as one of your best marketing tools. It is a way to provide a prospective employer a way to see positive things about you. Only post good photos and positive posts. Ya, I know I sound old, but this is important. The *Discovery Channel* found and recruited me through my *YouTube American Explosives Group* channel that landed me as a blaster on *Treasure Quest*. Use social media for good instead of being an annoyance. If your potential employer or client looks your name up on a computer, what will they see? If you do not know, you better have a look first!

It is all on the One Page
You are out and about and happen to meet someone that is ideal to be your next employer or client. Maybe an associate introduced you, so your foot is halfway in the door. You enjoy a positive conversation and exchange business cards. So now what? Often what happens is nothing and eventually the cards get tossed and an opportunity is lost. You want to keep that momentum going so they can keep you on top of their mind. When you get back to the office, you will want to email them a PDF copy of your resume, bio (for media related work) or a Company Capability Sheet for promoting a business.

Resumes should be simple, clean, and ideally down to one page. Bios should include video or page links to your work , music, or reels.

Company Capability Sheets should read like a short punchy resume for your business. Include licenses, special capabilities, special employees and high-profile clients. Anything to indicate why this is the company to hire now.

By having these documents ready on your computer or phone, you can send them off instantly and the recipient will be impressed with a short list of your accomplishments with options to contact you for a follow up. Include a short positive statement like, "Great to meet you today at ___. Attached is a PDF copy of my ___. I appreciate your time and I am looking forward to discussing the possibilities with you further. Thanks!"

Dress for Success

Next, you must look the part. Regardless of the profession, it is better to be slightly overdressed than underdressed, suiting up is even better. It has been said that shoes make the man or the woman. It's true, and my sound superficial, but in professional circles, you will be judged by what you are wearing and the shoes you have on.

On a budget? No problem. Many men and women sell or give away once expensive name brand clothing. Their careers are maybe winding down and they do not dress up like they did, or they just cannot fit into them anymore. Check online markets or resale clothing boutiques to get nice clothes at a fraction of the cost.

Take your new (used) name brand threads to the drycleaners and boom, they are new to you. No one needs to know the difference. When they compliment you on how nice you look, do not say you got the suit used, just smile, and say thank you. Your self-confidence will improve as you notice how others will treat you with more respect. They will call you sir or ma'am and open doors for you. You will do the same for them next time, it feels great to look and be professional.

Home and Auto

What about your car? Can you give someone a ride home from the office without your car covered in old cigarette butts and last week's fast-food cups and bags of garbage? If you are already a professional, your car should not look like the first one you have ever owned. I have driven old work trucks and Porsches and you do get more attention in a nicer car.

It is good to have a ride that matches your personality and your profession, but probably better not to drive something too flashy as it may look like an overcompensation. The vehicle should look like you are climbing up or have achieved success without the need to scream for attention.

How about your home? Can you entertain an important guest on a moment's notice? Can you have company over without the need to apologize for what a mess your place is in? Best to keep your house as if your boss or dream date is coming over in an hour. Need to entertain on a budget? No problem. Get a cheap drinkable bottle of wine and pour it into nice glasses. Take a frozen pizza and cut it into squares on a nice plate. Presentation is more impressive than the cost.

Be Ready to Travel

If your business could take you to another country, especially on short notice, check your passport. If you do not have one, consider ordering one now before you need it. It is less expensive than needing to rush one. They are good for ten years and most countries will want to see a year left before expiration to issue a travel visa.

Regardless of where you live, your next opportunity might be somewhere else. Be prepared to travel on short notice. That means a reliable vehicle, the ability to fly, good luggage and travel clothing. Traveling can also be expensive so it's a good idea to have funds or a backup credit card available in advance so you can be there for that job interview or business opportunity.

If you are meeting online through a video conference app like *Zoom* or *Skype*, make sure your background is appropriate. If you do not have a good background, consider dropping a greenscreen and selecting the background you like through the app. Be aware of background noise levels and lighting. Test video and audio first before the call.

Also be prepared to move if required to do so. Most do not like the idea of moving away from their home area, but it can be necessary to make the money you need to advance your career. Working on the road and moving your household can be expensive. It's a good idea to have funds available before you need them.

Checklist for Being Prepared:

Go through the checklist and mark off what you have completed. Make notes with a deadline on anything you still need to do to be ready:

[ ] A positive and confident mental attitude

_____

[ ] Cell phone outgoing message

_____

[ ] Professional email address

_____

[ ] Positive looking social media

_____

[ ] Social media video or page links for media or sports professionals

_____

[ ] Professional looking business cards

_____

[ ] Use professional photos, text, logos, and other media

_____

[ ] Updated Resume, Bio, or a Company Capability Statement

_____

[ ] Professional looking shoes and clothing

_____

[ ] Clean and reliable vehicle

_____

[ ] A home you can entertain someone in

_____

[ ] Passport if your business could take you to another country

_____

[ ] Finances available for travel to job interview or meeting

Anything else?

Just like the celebrities and big companies, build your brand. Maintain your reputation and be consistently good every day. Once your brand is established, the work is not finished, it is just getting started. You will need to protect your brand and help it grow. Let people find you and let them see you shine. It might just open the door to the dream opportunity you have been waiting for your entire life!

Who's Watching You?

You might not notice, but someone is watching you. Watching, listening, looking at your social media. Why? They are looking for someone just like you to be the next big thing. When you meet others, be 'on,' smile, and shake their hand like you mean it.

You just never know who you might meet and what they might positively impact your life. You never know how something you say and write could affect someone else. Maybe they tell their friends and associates, then introduce you to someone who can change your life, because you changed theirs.

The Least You Need to Know

- You are your own brand. Most do not think of brands neutrally, they are either positive or negative. How do others perceive you and why?

- People do judge a book by its cover. They will assume your personality and abilities match your appearance.

- Cleaning up your brand can be done quickly without spending much money.

- People like to be associated with name brands. They will spend money to promote the name and label. Think about what you can do to encourage others to promote you.

- The largest brands you can think of started with practically nothing. If they can do it, you can too.

- Once you are a name brand, you will attract attention, both positive and negative. Always think about ways to protect your brand.

- You never know how what you do, say, or write could affect someone else. Always be 'on' when you meet others, especially if someone is introducing you to someone they want you to meet. That person you are meeting could change your life because you can change theirs.

Chapter Four

Action 6. Do Not Fall Into Traps

Jeremy Whalen falling into a hidden tunnel in the Sacambaya jungle of Bolivia, South America in Discovery Channel's Treasure Quest.

We humans love our vices. We all have something we like to do or spend too much time or money on, perhaps. It could be anything from an obsessive hobby to a deadly illegal addition. No one is perfect and everyone has something they can work on. Is it bad to be obsessed? Well, no. The amazing energy that comes from obsession makes the world go around. The problem is when an obsession, vice or addiction turns into unproductive or unhealthy behavior.

Why is this so important? Because we only have so much time and money available to us within a day. We have a capacity of so many work hours and maybe even fewer highly productive or creative work hours where we can get the most completed. We also need to possibly balance our time with school, a day job, family and then our side hustle that will ideally turn into what we really want to do full time. Not to mention, we also need to take time to pursue objects of our desires, like someone we want to date or spend time with our spouse or partner.

There are also hobbies, friends, sports, keeping in shape, TV, the internet, music… the list goes on.

I know life can be extremely busy, but we all have the same hours in the day. This is why we need to have a balanced life of family, work and play, but I am also asking you to set aside time to work on deeply developing yourself, your brand and your business. This is not easy and most of us are not very good at it. To be effective we need to create time for ourselves by removing most of the other distractions. It is critical to free up enough time to improve our superpower and pursue our mission.

What do I mean by distractions and traps? Anything that wastes time and money to the point that it moves from a source of entertainment to an unhealthy addition. Distractions are one thing, but our modern landscape is riddled with landmines that, if you hit one, can require a lifetime of work to recover from. How do you know if you have fallen into a trap? The answer is simple. If the monkey you are fighting has, is, or will keep you from reaching your full potential.

If you cannot finish your education, keep a job, maintain friendships, a positive bank account or a sustain an intimate relationship, it might not always be 'them,' it might be 'you.' If things consistently crash around you, it is time to take ownership with a hard, honest look to see what is going on and what is holding you back. Or worse yet, cheating you from having a fulfilling and happy life.

Addictive Behavior

Some of us have an addictive personality. Some cannot eat a potato chip or two without devouring the whole bag. If something is good, we can use it all up and keep looking for more with no sense of moderation. My friend says he cannot go have a couple of beers. If he does, he will be the guy living under a bridge.

If you fall into this category and can recognize it, congratulations. If you have an addictive personality, you are more likely to fall into traps quicker and stay there longer. We see many people who have fallen in such deep traps they become the person living under a bridge or trying to jump off one. But not you, you will learn and know how to prevent this from happening. By being honest with yourself you can watch your actions and understand triggers that affect your behavior to stay ahead of the game.

Bad Habits to Deadly Additions

I do not have to list every vice here. There are plenty of examples you can think of on your own. Maybe one or two you are battling right now. Let me say this, it does not have to be illegal to be destructive. In the U.S., marijuana and video poker are legal in most states. These are legal because the states make money off them, but it does not mean they are a good idea.

Modern engineered pot is so strong, a couple hits of that and you will not get off the couch. That means you will not be doing much of anything else. There are also many cases of people with no more than a traffic ticket going to prison for embezzling from their employer after getting addicted to video poker and other forms of gambling. If you get fired, along with facing criminal charges from stealing from your employer, your career as you know it, is over.

What about smoking? Nicotine is so addictive, try smoking or chew a couple of times and you could be hooked for life. You have heard the warnings. You are paying to subject yourself to medical problems, possibly cancer and shorten your life. I must confess, I really enjoy cigars, but do not partake more than a few times of year because I don't want to become addicted.

If you really want to smoke, at least run the numbers to see what you are spending. Smoke one pack a day, $8 x 30 per month = $240 x 12 months = $2,880. That amount of money could fund a retirement account, make a car payment or allow you to take a nice family vacation. Instead you work hard your whole life, build wealth, have children, grandchildren, then die 15 years early from lung cancer? No one is immune to this. Walt Disney smoked up to three packs of cigarettes a day. This habit took the creative genius in the prime of his life, at the age of sixty-five. One day before the opening of Disney World in Florida.

Some drugs are so addictive, use them once and you are hooked for life. Opioids, heroin, meth, do you think that anyone can use these and just stop without serious consequences to their physical, mental and spiritual health? For those who get hooked on these drugs, it is not a matter of going to one program to get clean. It is a struggle with recovery for decades with serious damage to your health, relationships, finances, and spiritual wellbeing.

You definitely will not be doing much to distinguish yourself in a positive way. I am telling you all of this so you will stop and think before falling into any series addictive traps. It so much easier not to start then spending a lifetime trying to recover from their poison.

To Drink or Not to Drink

I had an interesting conversation with a minister friend. He said the sin is not in having a drink, it is getting drunk and being stupid. I also had a police officer friend tell me that seeing people drunk after midnight is always trouble. "Nothing good can come from it." I could not agree more. Some people do not, but most people do. Especially in business-related social events. Most are drinking and often there are open bars where you have the opportunity to drink as much as you'd like without the bar tab. This temptation to keep from drinking requires discipline.

If alcoholism is in your family history or you have an addictive personality, better not to even start. If you are out at a social event, there is no problem in having a cola or juice in a glass on the rocks and no one needs to know if you are drinking or not. It's not their business. If you do drink, do not get intoxicated in public. Nothing can tank your career faster than getting drunk and belligerent at a work-related social event. I have seen the most promising young executives set themselves back with embarrassing antics, or worse, get into a fight or sleep with the wrong person. Many years of hard work can be erased in a moment of stupidity.

Then, to add insult to injury, get a DUII on the way home. Once out of jail, you will be in an expensive legal entanglement that can prevent you from being insured and possibly being able to drive, drive for work or driving a company vehicle. Either way, nothing good can come from it. Managing alcohol will make you appear responsible. Being a bad drunk will make you look foolish and someone who lacks self-control.

Fighting Depression

Everyone from time to time can get the blues. Many like veterans, have *Post Traumatic Stress Disorder*. Some are depressed at times, others are chronic. It seems that many that are chronically depressed are that way due to the constant onslaught of negative self-talk such as, "*I will never feel better,*" or "*Nothing will ever work out for me.*" This accompanied with other negative input such as dark movies and music, are the perfect self-fulfilling prophesy of doom and gloom.

I can offer the clique' of "Think Positive," but you know that if you are suffering from depression, it will take something more than that. Like the example of imagining your ideal life in the Introduction, dreaming, or thinking positive alone will not get you there. It does however provide a path in your brain so you can see what is possible. We are not going to chase a dream we cannot see, let alone imagine would even be possible.

So, now I am telling you know think positive in a way that will help you imagine a way out, an alternative to the situation you are in. Zoom out of your problems and see the bigger picture. It is like looking at a maze, from your point of view all you see is walls. When you get a larger overhead view you can clearly see a way out to freedom. You know what is next. That's right, time for action.

If you need professional help, get it. There is no shame in it, and no one needs to know. It is very therapeutic to talk to someone. At least talk to family and friends. Don't isolate yourself, it will only make it worse. Having time to yourself only provides you more time to get deeper into your head with negative talk. Now is the time to get another perspective and advice that will help you. Find someone else who has navigated out of the maze and ask them how they did it.

One of my best friends had created a large portfolio of rental properties. He turned to gambling as a way to relieve the stress of a demanding job. He was addicted to cards and soon rang up debt he felt he could no longer pay off. He never told anyone how depressed he was. He appeared happy and fun loving, but on the inside, he must have been in unbearable pain.

We did not know how much pain until we got a call on Christmas Day that he had taken his own life. When someone lets this level of depression escalate to suicide, it does not only affect them but everyone around them. Ripples of sadness from this tragedy are still felt a decade later.

Understand that life works in tides and seasons. The ocean has a high and low tides every day. There are four seasons in a year. If you are experiencing a low tide in the cold darkness of winter, remember the big picture and keep things in prospective. High tide and Spring are coming up next. Throughout a day or a week there are times we will feel up, down, productive, creative, and lazy.

When you are having a productive time, run with it. Get as much done as you can. When you are feeling down, remember, it is just low tide, you will rise again soon.

"We may walk through the Valley of the Shadow of Death, but we don't live there. We are not going to pitch our tent there, we are just passing through." That is a quote from Pastor Robert Cox, of *Bethel Baptist Church* in Hawthorne, Nevada. Hard times do pass, and even faster the sooner we take action to resolve the crisis. No victim or negative self-talk.

Worry and action take about the same about of energy. Do something to improve yourself and your situation right now. Don't wait, right now. Saying you will do it later, tomorrow, January 1st, whenever, just gives you time to stall and back out. Make a simple plan. Maybe write down three simple things then get off the couch and do them one at a time.

Ultimately, the best way to deal with this problem is to head full throttle into what you were made to do. There is little time to worry or get into your head to tell yourself you cannot do something if you are already doing it. Doing, learning how to achieve, eventually becoming successful, that is that best therapy going.

Crime Does Not Pay

In a past career, I took a job for the *Oregon State Judicial Department* to help create a program to manage criminal defendants who were charged with new crimes, released from jail, but not yet convicted. The problem being a high percentage did not bother to go back to court costing more tax dollars to have these defendants arrested and run back through a court system they were too intoxicated to show up for.

Over the years I got to meet and know hundreds of criminals from all walks of life. Some small time, some big time, gang members, drug dealers, sex offenders, scam artists, identity and financial thieves, you name it. One thing they all had in common is they never got anything out of their criminal endeavors. Some dealers and thieves would make a little money on a short-term basis, but ultimately, they always got caught, imprisoned, hospitalized, or dead. I never met one who got rich, let alone make any consistent money that was worth all the pain and suffering they put themselves and their families through.

Another real concern is that once you are 18, you are an adult and criminal convictions are on your record for life. One stupid moment of youthful indiscretion and it will haunt you for decades. Once you have a drug charge, violent crime, or a felony on your record, you have extremely limited who can or will hire you.

One of my best friends was about 18 when he and a couple of buddies got drunk and decided to push a parked car down a hill for fun. The time the car made it to the bottom of the hill, tens of thousands of dollars of damage had been done. The guys got caught, convicted of felonies, and had to pay restitution for all the damage they caused.

My friend wanted to be a police officer, but that career path ended. Do not do anything that will risk your reputation, freedom, or career. Instead of buying a sports car, he had to make payments to the court. Later he had to pay an attorney to have his felony expunged so he could vote and purchase a firearm. One moment changed his career path with consequences throughout his life.

Love, Marriage and Children

I once read a sign in a Baja Mexico bar, "Love is Grand, Divorce is 100 Grand." That about sums it up. If you are going to get married, it is a lot cheaper to stay married. Easier said than done however, as half of the marriages in the U.S. end in divorce. I'm not just quoting a statistic, I have been there and been divorced twice. If you want to be married, choose carefully, it is just too expensive and emotionally draining to go through a divorce. Who suffers the most are the children involved. They pay the price for their parent's poor choices.

Consider this, if you are rising in your career, find a partner based not where you are now, but where you will be in five years. Make sure that person understands how hard you need to work to get where you want to be. They will need patience and understanding with you going to college, working long hours, and possibly traveling to propel your career.

If they tell you it is not worth the work or sacrifice, and you should just hang out with them to watch TV, it is not going to work. Stay away from negative, insecure, uninspired, over dramatic or anyone who cannot keep up with you or tries to hold you back. Save time, money, and heartache now. Take your walking papers and move on.

Once you get to where you want to be, socially and financially, you will meet more people in your same lane. Higher on the food chain, people working to improve their lives, to rise and achieve, instead of soul sucking swirling drama. They say opposites attract, I do not think they were talking about long-term commitment and marriage.

Find someone that you share many similarities with. Be on the same page when it comes to the big issues like sex, children, money, and religion. I know that finding the perfect someone is not easy to do, but there is no rush. Enjoy the search and the journey of getting to know someone who you might be compatible with.

Just as there is no rush to get married, I also feel that there is no rush to have children. Do not get me wrong, I am a father and love my children more than anything. It has been said there is no perfect time to have kids, I disagree. Having children when you are ready to have them in a loving marriage is ideal.

Yes, I said married, because you know ladies, that if you are not, a man can walk away and leave you hanging. I have seen ladies drop out of college because they had an 'unexpected' pregnancy. To make matters worse, it was by men who they were not in love with or would take responsibility for children. Both men and women need to take 100% responsibility for this. No excuses. There are a half dozen ways not to get pregnant. If you are having unprotected sex, you will have babies. There's nothing unexpected about it.

I am not telling you all of this as some kind of old prude guy. I understand the importance of sex, love, marriage, and children. I have raised my three kids during times of financial difficulty while going to school and working long hours and have admired many single mothers who juggle these things also.

The stress can take its toll on relationships, and ultimately the children pay the price when they hear parents yelling at each other and Dad moving out. Take your time, be selective and have children when you and your mate are ready. I am telling you it is better to be able to focus and have fun with your kids than passing them off to a babysitter because you need to work to pay the rent.

Sexual Harassment and Dating Co-Workers
Nothing will destroy your career faster than engaging in or even being accused of sexual harassment.

34

There are examples in the news on an ongoing basis of some of the wealthiest and powerful men in the world being accused of this. All their money, power, influence, and legal teams cannot help them. They still get fired, get sued, even go to prison. Your employer does not want to spend tens of thousands of dollars defending a lawsuit over someone's bad behavior. It's easier, cheaper, and more socially acceptable to fire you in a blink of any eye. Advising you to behave yourself seems obvious, but this problem takes so many men down, some ground rules must be revisited:

- Do not get drunk at company events
- Do not take advantage of drunk co-workers
- Do not make comments about someone's body type or features
- Do not make sexual comments or jokes
- Do not make advances to co-workers, clients, or associates
- Do not have sexual relations with anyone you work with
- Do not even date anyone you work with

Yes, do not even date anyone who you work with or have some professional connection to. I know it is tempting and people do it all the time because we tend to be drawn to people we spend time with. Sometimes it is hard not to fall for someone who we find attractive and see every working day. Just do not do it. Whether it turns into dating or a full relationship, if you break up, nothing good will come from it. You will both create a great deal of drama, and one or both could be fired or need to leave the job.

Trade a Vice for a Positive Alternative

Quitting a bad habit cold turkey is not easy. In fact, it is almost impossible. One trick that is often helpful is to look at trading one habit for another. We choose bad habits because they typically give us some form of temporary pleasure. For example, cigarettes are popular because the nicotine is a stimulant. When smoking you get a little buzz to the brain. It might provide a minor stimulus that makes it enjoyable and highly addictive.

But consider working out. Exercise can also provide much of the same feeling. Working out releases natural hormones that can make you feel even better, *Runner's High*.

These include: *Adrenaline*, pleasure, strength and stress control, *Endorphins*, a pain killer, *Serotonin*, a mood stabilizer, *Oxytocin*, pleasurable feeling released during sex and *Dopamine*, providing a rewarding pleasurable sensation.

So, let us consider the two activities. Both provide a stimulant and make you feel good, but smoking provides a risk of many medical problems. Eventually, cancer can take over a decade off your life. Exercise can give you a high feeling, improves your physical health, muscle tone and appearance as well as your mental health, energy, memory and overall wellbeing. Trading exercise for smoking is a clear win-win.

Another example is a friend of mine who enjoyed on-line gambling and video poker. Doing so provides some of the same feel-good hormones in the rare circumstances when you win. Consider the alternative of buying stocks. This can be done on-line and involves some of the same strategies. You pick your best choices and watch the value increase or decrease.

Now let us look at the overall long-term consequences. For video poker, the average payout is approximately 97% percent. The house or machine gets at least 3% or more, leaving the player what is left. Invest $100 at get back $97 if you are lucky. Because the need to win is so psychologically strong, most players let any winnings ride until eventually most of the money is gone.

How about stocks? The average return is 10% Yes, they go up and down and you could lose, but over the long-term they pay off at least 10%. Invest the same $100 and get a $110 return and enjoy the same pleasurable winning feelings because you picked or helped pick the profitable stocks. So, playing stocks, can still be risky, but overall a positive alternative to gambling.

Ditch Your Bad Habits While You Are Still Poor
Because it is so difficult to break a bad habit, I am hoping I can catch some of you before you pick up any serious vices that could derail your mission. Remember this quote by Zig Ziglar, "You don't have to get out of trouble you don't get into."

If you have fallen into a trap, it is important to get a handle on your vice now. Why? It is critical for two reasons.

First, you will have difficulty reaching your full potential if you need to spend much of your time and money battling vices and addictions. Second, as you become more successful, you could have much more money and a more flexible schedule. The combination of more money and flexible time allows you and your amateur additions to turn pro. Get your house in order before you get into real trouble.

What Are Your Triggers?

Most of us get into trouble because some condition has encouraged us to take an action that we might not normally do. Know that you are not alone. As humans, we are perfectly imperfect beings all struggling with much of the same emotions. Consider what triggers you might have that could lead to harmful addictive behavior?

[ ] Boredom
[ ] Loneliness
[ ] Rejection
[ ] Depression
[ ] Anxiety
[ ] Uncertainty
[ ] Failure
[ ] Peer Pressure
[ ] _____

When you are experiencing these negative emotional triggers, what can you do instead of engaging in harmful addictive behavior?

[ ] Call a friend or family member
[ ] Intimacy with a loved one
[ ] Exercise
[ ] Pray or meditate
[ ] Get outside
[ ] Enjoy a hobby
[ ] Leisure time
[ ] _____

The Least You Need to Know

- Understand that you must be extra careful If you have an addictive personality or addiction is hereditary.

- Certain behaviors like video poker, cigarettes or heroin are so addictive, try them once and you can be hooked for life.

- Understand that waiting to have children until after you are married, then staying married, are two of the biggest life factors in keeping you out of poverty and raising successful children.

- One of the best ways to fight depression is to do what you are meant to do in life. It is hard to be depressed when you are reaching self-actualization.

- Quitting an addiction cold turkey is extremely difficult. Look at a more healthy substitute behavior.

- Do not harass, date, or have sex with co-workers.

- Learn to recognize any possible negative triggers that could encourage you to engage in harmful addictive behavior.

- Get your vices in check before you have extra time and money. Without financial limitation, your bad habits will only become worse.

Chapter Five

Action 5. Learn to Communicate

Jack training Indian Army Special Forces troops, Hanan, India.

Nothing will affect your success more than the ability to communicate. This is true in business, your personal life, activities like sports and in your relationships. Think back to any of these areas where you remember a conflict in your own life. Chances are the problem was created from a lack of communication, then became progressively worse as the talking became more abrasive or just stopped.

Once you understand that poor communication creates most problems, you will be able to recognize this faster to step in and possibly provide a bridge to solve the issue. Good communication skills typically do not come naturally. They are learned and practiced. We will review a number of tools that will help you immediately.

What Are You Telling Yourself?

Out of all the conversations you have throughout the day, the person you talk with most is yourself. Now is the time to consciously hear what you are saying and how you are saying it within your own head. Is what you are affirming positive or negative? Do you encourage yourself or criticize yourself? Understand that if you are telling yourself you can or cannot do something, you are absolutely right. Self-talk is a complete self-fulfilling prophecy.

When you review a problem in your head, do you break it down into pieces to determine the best way to solve it? Or is it the worst thing ever and life will never the same? Understand the way you interact with yourself matters. The words you choose and how you frame issues within your own mind. It is critical to understand what you are saying to yourself before you are effective in communicating with anyone else.

One of my mentors, Coach Bill Ballester says, "You get what you focus on." You focus on excellence, being positive and finding solutions, you get more excellence, positivity and solutions. You focus on excuses and negativity and everything is a crisis. No surprise-you get more excuses, negativity, and crisis.

This rule applies to both internal and external communication. Self-affirmations have been beat to death by motivational speakers and turned into a joke on *Saturday Night Live*. However, no joke. Sometimes you really need to pump yourself up. It is an integral part of self-confidence. If I have a challenge, I remember a past time where I took action to overcome a similar challenge. It's how I work with high explosives, perform in front of a movie camera, or step onto a stage in front of hundreds of people. "I have been here before. I know how to do this. I will exceed expectations. I can do this again!"

If you need self-confidence and cannot say anything positive to yourself, that is okay, you will. Once you learn and move forward in your career, you will develop life experiences that will give you confidence as you overcome more challenges. Choose your tone and worlds carefully when you self-talk. See what a difference it makes.

Sell the Idea

One of the most important ways to communicate is to let someone else know your intention or idea. Many have great ideas, but they are afraid to let their opinion or voice be heard. Everyone has ideas, some are certainly better than others but what is interesting is that many good ideas were turned down over and over. As an example, the television series *Survivor* and the movie series *Star Wars* were both turned down by many networks and studios. Mark Burnett and George Lucas along with their associates had to keep pitching and selling the ideas until someone finally said yes.

Before you can sell your idea to someone, you need to convince yourself. Ask yourself what makes your idea a good one.

What questions or objections would someone have to it? Think like a trial attorney to anticipate how someone might respond. That lets you plan how to address possible reactions. Practice pitching the main concept then break it down to three or fewer ways to implement it. Be open to constructive ideas from others on how your idea could be made better. Once your idea is being considered and reviewed by others, you can orchestrate the collaboration in making it better, more relevant and implementation.

Make Plans

Anytime you see a group a people together in a work situation with the absence of leadership it is typically quite a cluster. Some will be sitting around talking while others will be rushing off in the attempt to haphazardly get something accomplished. This pattern often fits our intuition to rush and race, then possibly making a plan later. My associates and I have studied high-functioning team development and by far the most product teams stop, set a goal, make a plan, delegate tasks, then get on with getting it done.

Whether you are officially in charge or not, you can take charge by helping groups with this exercise until they become more focused and efficient. Remember what we just covered in selling your idea? Well, now is the time to present viable ideas and get buy-in from others to get the job done. If you are in charge already, no problem. But what if you are not? Not only do you have to sell the idea to get others to agree, you need to do so in a way that is diplomatic. Bosses do not like employees who step on their toes and employees can take offence to being told what to do by someone who is not over them.

This is where language is important. Language and diplomacy. "Due to this situation, maybe we could all consider doing the job this way?" The word *consider* is non-threatening. You are not saying we must do it my way, you are saying let us think about doing it my way and here's why. When it comes to you delegating work to lateral staff, you can pick a job as challenging as any other and offer to do that yourself. If you need help, ask who you want to help you. If the others are unsure what to do, you can suggest tasks for them to do while you are doing your job. "Joe, will you help me with doing ____, if you guys want to do ____?"

The language I chose in this example is reasonable and not confrontational. It is exercising leadership and not just demanding how to do something and who should do it.

41

Do not worry about getting the credit. Once people understand you have good ideas, they will come to you to ask for more.

Once they realize you know how to lead people, and turn ideas into plans, they will keep asking you regardless if you are the boss or not. Remember the goal here is to distinguish yourself and show others you can lead, build teams, manage by objectives, and get things done. This is how you can help fast track from employee to supervisor.

Remember Names

In your personal and profession life you will meet many people. The more your career advances, the number will increase and the more important they will become. When meeting people it seems the moment we are introduced, and shake their hand, our brain blacks out. For whatever reason we get nervous or overwhelmed at just the moment the person gives us their name and what they do. We need to practice staying focused, listen and remember what they are telling us. Repeat their name and try using some form of association so you can match the name to the person. Remembering a name is a great way to impress someone so they remember you. Stay focused during the introduction. Practice meeting people until you get good at it.

Sometimes you meet so many people, you just cannot remember everyone, then you have the awkward moment when you need to introduce them to someone else. You hope that when you state the person's name you know, it will trigger them to state their name. After the conversation, use your notes page in your phone to type in the name and how they are associated.

This gives you a fighting chance to remember them later, or the old fashion way, offer to exchange business cards. Practice by deliberately remembering the name of someone while you are out at the gas station, restaurant, bank and grocery store. Greet them by their name and smile. They will be nicer to you and when you meet a CEO at the next business outing, you will remember the name.

Once or twice, I have used, "How do pronounce your name?" Like you have known it all along, but just forgot how to pronounce it. Yes, it's corny, but it works for difficult names and it is less socially awkward then saying you forget. So, when she says, "Tammy." You can say, "Oh I thought maybe it pronounced *Tammy~?*" It might get a chuckle. Besides making fun of yourself is an easy exit out of an awkward social interaction.

When entering a social gathering, instead of thinking 'Here I am,' say, "There you are!" And greet them by their name. The beginning of any human interaction is a greeting with names. Practice this until you nail it. Few things will distinguish you more.

Confident and Funny

Communication is all about great interpersonal human interaction allowing your personality to shine through. If you are shy and lack self-confidence, that's okay. Social interaction is a skill that can be learned and improved on. Great speakers, entertainers and comedians don't always have natural talent. They get in front of a mirror and practice like anyone else working on improving their art.

So, what makes an interesting personality that naturally draws in others? Start with being confident and funny. No not bloviate, babble or embellish to the point of lying. People will see through this quickly. Use intelligence, wit and charm and you are suddenly sexy and intriguing. Think more *James Bond* instead of *Barney Fife.* Every action and word has purpose, initiated with class and style. Soon you could be the most interesting person in the room.

When I say be confident, I mean self-assured, not arrogant or too cocky. You smile, are friendly, and are comfortable in your own skin. You are deliberate in your actions and everything you do or say has reason. Be funny, too. You might be asking is that really necessary? Using appropriate humor breaks the ice, allows others to enjoy you, be comfortable around you, and more importantly, remember you.

Approach humor with caution. You are not the class clown or court jester. It is not your job to entertain everyone, but it does not hurt to make them smile. Watch comedians on how they get laughs. They look for targets they can use or exaggerate about to make a clever point or make fun of. They also look for props and use timing.

Here is a way to practice having fun with humor. The next time you are in line at the grocery store, have a look at the person ahead of you and pick a couple things they are buying to come up with a joke. Try it, you will soon find yourself grinning like an idiot while standing in line. The reason for this is teaching you to be witty and clever in the moment. Nothing is canned, you come up with something humorous and interesting from the opportunity that is before you.

43

One day shopping I was in a mood and decided to try it for real. A beautiful woman in line ahead of me was buying frozen shrimp and motor oil. With a straight face I asked, "How does that work? I have always just used butter and garlic?" Her social shield was up and on full, but my dumb joke was able to get through. Her stern look turned into a smile, then a laugh that sparked a conversation. We were having so much fun the grocery checker and another giggling person in line joined in the conversation. Think of personal interactions like short stories. They have a beginning, middle and end. I say personal interactions because we are not robots with canned speeches.

We are humans with personalities and emotions. Keep it real, nothing creepy or weird. People can see fake a mile away, like someone coming at you with the latest pyramid scheme. Be friendly, be genuine and enjoy the experience of meeting and getting to know others. If you are an extrovert, this might sound like fun, but for an introvert, the idea could be terrifying.

Acting Lessons

Ever notice that conversations in the movies are not that similar to real life conversations? Movie dialog is typically smoother, cleaner and more deliberate. Real life conversations are more based from not listening, than people talking over each other. Would you like to communicate like your favorite actor or actress? Taking acting lessons may not be as crazy as it sounds.

Here is an example. Good communication is not just memorizing and repetitively practicing the same lines. Good actors bring life to the role and the drama being played out. This is done through emotion, feeling, circumstances and more importantly, playing off the other person. Listening, then meaningfully responding at just the right time instead of "walking over them" with a canned speech. Actors also 'block out' their actions by planning in advance where and how they are physically moving and when to deliver their lines. This keeps them from looking like they are just stumbling around on set.

One popular and effective style is Method Acting. This is when the actor psychologically assumes the role of the character they are portraying. They create an emotional attachment where they feel, think and operate under the same motivational influences. Using this system well means even taking on the subconscious behavior of the character.

I used method acting when doing reality TV for *Treasure Quest*. Essentially it was easy because I was playing myself. The role was already assumed, and I would speak and respond like I would just being myself. Well, you are playing your own role too.

Whatever that role is, you need to assume it, own it and act like who you are supposed to be. We have seen people who based upon their status or position, we expect to act to certain standard, but they do not. Something seems or feels off, by them not living up or acting to the expectations we have placed on them. Well, no one is perfect, and we do tend to raise influential and celebrity personalities to demigod levels that no one could completely live up to.

This does, however, give us much to consider. Are we living up to the role we have assumed? We want titles, responsibilities, influence, but are we still comfortable about acting like a total idiot? Others do this so well, their quiet confidence makes you think that they own half of the world whether they do or not. My point is good actors are good actors for a reason, they have completely assumed the role they are playing.

They are so good it is hard to believe they are not really doctors or action heroes. If fact, if you met them in public, you might not be surprised if they saved the life of a choking person or single handedly took out the bad guy. They are playing for money. So are you, although the critical difference is this is your real life. You need to assume your role so deeply, no one will question you on your knowledge or competence.

Before each scene, the director yells, "Action!" Throughout this book you will notice I am yelling this at you too- Action! The lights are on and the camera is rolling. That is your que to get off your arse and move! You will be defined not by the role you take, but by the action you take while in your role:

If you want to be smart, act smart.
If you want to be great, act great.
If you want to be confident, act confident.
If you want to be brave, act brave.
If you want to be caring, act caring.

You get the idea. It is all about acting out actions.

If you want to be loved, love someone else.
If you want to create, start creating something.
If you want knowledge, you must start learning.
If you want to be trusted, you must learn to trust someone else.
If you want faith, you must start believing.
If you want success, you must act until you have earned it.
If you want money, you must act like you can manage it.

You might feel like you cannot do any of these things. That is okay. Remember actors cannot either, but they do it anyway because they have assumed the role. They fake it until they feel it. You must do that also. Just get in the game and be conscious of how you are acting. How do others perceive you? You are not what you say you are, you are what you act like you are.

Practice Clothes Shopping

Time to practice having a go with some real face-to-face. There are people who get paid to talk with you. Start with them first. Remember the encounter needs a beginning, middle and end. It is time to update your wardrobe. Get dressed up in some of the best clothes you have already and go to a shopping mall clothing department. Find an approachable sales representative and looking for their name tag.

Begin the conversation with a smile and eye contact. "Hi ___, my name is ___, could you help me?" If you use someone's first name and honestly ask for help, it is nearly impossible for them to say no. "I have an important event coming up, a dinner party at my bosses' house and I need to update my business casual. Can you help me pick some items out? Not the most expensive, but they cannot look cheap either. My event is important, so I need to look good."

Notice everything about the question has purpose. You are on mission to look good for a company event. You are a serious buyer and have even set a price range. The salesperson is also happy they were addressed by their name and that you are asking their personal opinion to help.

The salesperson is now willing to work hard for you because you are not there to waste time and they think you already trust their fashion judgement. Congratulations. Your new friend is now motivated to help you look good. After they help you, thank them again by name and shake their hand while reminding them of your name. They will remember you next time and will give you first class treatment.

You will not distinguish yourself by being bashful, hiding in the corner and not making conversation. You need to get out and be socially interactive. Be confident, funny, charming, intelligent and interesting. Oh ya, well-dressed too. Practice until you are dialed in. No pressure, but the next person you meet could be the love of your life or someone who can hire you and change your life.

Finding Similarities

We have been told about Diversity. Diversity might make us different and unique. That is great but understand the glue that holds us all together is not our differences. It is our similarities. One of the best ways to build report with someone is to focus on what you have in common. Even people from completely different walks of life share some of the same beliefs and ideas. Search out those topics you can agree on.

Business level common interests can include:
>   The overall company mission
>   Tactical objectives to help reach the overall mission
>   Daily objective goals to achieve tactical objectives

Personal level common interests can include:
>   Education
>   Children
>   Music and Movies
>   Religion
>   Politics
>   Hobbies

Find similarities. Make a friend. Who knows? You might have enough in common you become business associates, or friends, for life.

To Cuss or Not to Cuss

Do not do it, it sounds like sh*t! Seriously, because everyone can do it or does do it, it is not impressive. Even some women talk like drunk sailors which sometimes is a little surprising. It does not make you sound tough and it does not make you sound smart. Besides, depending on how bad the words are, a kitten or possibly a puppy is going to die.

You will notice people that have the highest intelligence or the most authority, do not cuss, yell, or scream. Their actions including the words they choose show compete self-control. This book is about how to distinguish yourself, and I have found that you tend to stand out more by not cussing. I have been asked why I do not cuss. Not cussing can give the appearance of intelligence and control.

I must confess, there are times I cuss, even drop the F-bomb, however I try to reserve that language for hitting my thumb with a hammer moment. I have spent plenty of time on construction sites, mine sites auto garages, and other guy-dominated work areas. Is it okay to cuss there? If you get in the habit of cussing, it is hard to stop. It will be a roadblock to your career. Let us say you are a line worker and your supervisor would like to move you into management.

Yes, you are moving up. You even get your own office with secretarial staff and other office personnel. The problem is you cannot put two sentences together with cussing four times. How is that going to work? Do you expect your supervisor to advance you if you could embarrass them by sounding low class or offending office personnel?

Language used sets the professionalism, mood, and tone of the environment. Every word used should be positive and constructive. If you take a dirt road to salty words, it can appear as if you are uneducated or have lost control of your emotions. Understand also, that as a leader, your people will talk the way you do. If you make bad language acceptable, they will be happy to use it also.

Does this sound strict? Yes. And do you have to follow this advice? No. The idea here however is to distinguish yourself, not to sound like you are fresh out of prison. Use language that is becoming of a lady or gentlemen. Someone who is in charge with wisdom and authority. Do everything and say everything with class and style.

Gang Land

I once worked on a blasting site with a young man who was a hardcore gang member. He had felony convictions but worked hard to turn his life around. He left his former life of crime, got married, and started a family. He worked hard to get a construction job and worked even harder to work his way up within the company.

One of the things he told me is that he had to learn to speak proper English.

I was taken back. You assume that someone can speak the language, but it's not the case if you grow up in an environment were the only language you know is gangster slang. Some business people act like gangsters, but they do not sound like street thugs. My friend knew he had to re-train himself to speak proper English, and he did.

He wanted to be a blaster, however his criminal history might not let him. He was a hardworking and likeable guy. I wanted to help him for these reasons. It is amazing how many others will offer to help someone once they see them help themselves. The reason for this is simple. No one wants a losing investment. If they are going to throw in for someone or something, they want some assurance that there will be a winning outcome.

It's a Test

I have helped negotiate a hundred small business transactions and have been in few romantic relationships. Interestingly enough, business transactions and romantic relationships tend to follow the same interpersonal path. There is a courtship where the parties meet, get to know each other, and decide what level of business they will do together. On a personal level that means if they are going to be acquaintances, friends, love interests, or marriage. One thing I have noticed, more often than not, when things are getting serious someone says, "No."

When I was helping negotiate small business transactions, a potential buyer might submit a letter of intent or a purchase offer, then somewhere in the process the deal would crash. Something would happen with financing or a clash of personalities. Then after much work, the deal was off. As a broker it is difficult to watch because the money from the commission on the sale that had already been spent in my head, just drifted away into thin air.

After a while I learned to get off the emotional rollercoaster and realize that 'no' was just part of the normal course of the dance.
I have learned to see 'no' as a test. When one party says 'no,' maybe they want to see how you will react. It is a way to determine the commitment level of the parties. It also provides a break in the negotiations to step back and evaluate the deal. Take another non-emotional look to evaluate what it's worth to you. What additional money is needed or contingencies met before the deal is back on the table to CPR it back to life? Maybe everyone walks away or maybe they put in the extra effort seeing the value of the transaction.

49

Couples do this too. Possibly before an engagement, they take a break to evaluate the relationship. Maybe it is a good arrangement, maybe it's not, but at least you are not emotionally rushing into something. I think taking a pause is a good idea. My dad told me once when I was a kid to sleep on the idea of spending my savings on a toy remote-control car. It was a good advice because the following year I spent the same money for a down payment on a real car.

Ultimately, life is about agreements. The better agreements, business transactions, and personal relationships, the better your life will be. Remember not to overreact when you hear 'no.' Smile, breathe, and use your communication skills and everything else you have learned to determine how to proceed.

Difficult People

Life is full of difficult people. There is no way around it. The finest families and companies are full of them. These people will challenge all of your communication abilities. I have seen it all. On the low end, bad attitudes, bullying, lying, escalating to fighting, stealing, and criminal behavior. One bad person can quickly disrupt the whole team until the drama is spinning out of control. I have seen leadership let this happen and it is ridiculous for bad behavior to be tolerated, especially in a professional environment.

As a specialized small team guy, I do not like dysfunctional or difficult people. Dysfunctional people will suck the life energy out of you until you are exhausted. I would down an energy drink to run away from them faster. When it is up to me, I go through an extended evaluation process utilizing references to help ensure I don't hire anyone who doesn't fit. I would rather take the extra time to find the right person than to take someone who does not fit, and then try to make them fit. Honestly, this is almost impossible and often an exercise in beating your head into a wall. Be patient and ask your associates to help recruit or recommend the right candidate.

Sometimes you do not get a choice. Possibly they are in a government agency where no one gets fired or a family member you can't vote off the island. Conflict comes from failed expectations. You have high expectations for yourself and you expect others to care as well. I consider this the leader's responsibility to make sure everyone knows what the mission is and what expectations there are to ensure that it gets done.

It is all about communication from the top down. We should not assume everyone knows the mission or what they need to do to achieve it.

It is up to leadership to sell the mission. If people do not want to do it, leadership needs to find someone who is motivated for the opportunity. If they are willing, but can't, then the question is, are they trainable? Sometimes you can bring people around if you can sell them on the big picture. Remind them of the mission that is bigger than any one person. Why you are there, how important it is, and what similarities you share. Then provide the proper training needed to get them on track.

If someone is not interested, willing, or trainable, it is time to let them go. Why spend valuable resources on the unwilling? It gets worse. While some may be uninterested or unwilling, some others are bullies, toxic, or straight up criminals. One bad person can distract, poison and will eventually throw off the entire organization. It is clearly better not to even have them there. Any work they provide will probably come back and bite you later.

Some toxic people find enjoyment at creating as many problems as possible. They lie, cheat, scheme and bully, but when you stand up to them and call them out, they play victim. They want you to lose your temper and control, maybe even punch them so they can file a lawsuit. As someone who will or already does lead people, you need to be ready for this. Be ready for anything. Everyone encounters drama and dramatic, difficult people. The critical thing is how you react to it. If someone wants to you to cuss, scream, and fight, don't take the bait. Be calm, professional, and the one in charge.

You will have a greater effect on the toxic people by taking out a pen and paper and writing down everything they are doing and saying. Document everything. I once failed to do so, and it can turn into your word against theirs. Do not fall for that. People know who the troublemaker is, you just might have to prove it. My attorney friend told me that the party that wins in court is the one with the most documentation.

Ask How to Do it Better
NEWS stands for North, East, West and South and the old news adage was: Who, What, Why and When? A good reporter's job was to ask questions then report what they discovered on a story.

Now it seems that news agencies and people in general have forgotten to ask questions and instead operate on information assumed or what has been provided for them.

The best way to learn, influence and lead people is to ask questions. Like, "Why do you do it this way?" Or, "What is your input on doing this job more efficiently?" We should be asking ourselves the same questions while we are at it. By doing so, we learn valuable information on how to make things even better.

Equally important, you are developing a culture where co-workers are encouraged to be engaged to be innovative and contribute to the good of the organization. This makes those around you stake holders in the cause and not just employees. People are competitive by nature with the impulse to keep potentially useful information to themselves. When we get to contribute, we can go from an employee mindset to one of an important stakeholder.

Leaders remind others that we are all working on the same team to help them become collaborative instead of competitive. When associates freely share useful information on how to do something better, that is when the magic happens. Real innovation that allows you to leapfrog over problems and worn out technology. Collaborative innovation has an exciting multiplying effect as people contribute ideas to make something better than any one person on their own could imagine.

People often know how to do something more efficiently, safer, for less money, but they may not be willing to tell you unless you ask them. Will every suggestion you get be a winner? No. But you will discover ideas that maybe you had not thought of and implement them. Watch morale soar when you give credit to the people who provided them. Let them know that their ideas and input have value and you trust them to collaborate and contribute.

This communication business is so critical because nothing will affect the quality of your life more than who you meet and the relationships you foster. It all starts with a smile. "Hello, my name is…" Then it evolves into, "Why do we do it this way and how can we do it even better?"

What Can You Do to Become a Better Communicator?

Knowing how important this is, get to work now to improve your skills. Here are some actions that will help:

[ ] Smile more often
[ ] Become a better listener
[ ] Let the other party talk without cutting them off
[ ] Stop being so bashful
[ ] Ask smart questions
[ ] Be aware of your body language
[ ] Take a genuine interest in what others are telling you
[ ] Find opportunities to let your sense of humor come through
[ ] Focus on similarities or what you have in common
[ ] Enjoy flirting in a tactful way
[ ] Reduce babble, engage brain before mouth
[ ] Remove noise and distractions that prevent you from hearing
[ ] Learn to mirror the other person with similar tone and actions
[ ] _____

The Least You Need to Know

- Nothing will affect your success in your business and personal life more than the ability to communicate.

- The first aspect of communication is awareness of what you are telling yourself. Your self-talk creates the self-fulfilling prophecy of self-doubt or self-confidence.

- Be prepared to sell your idea. Just because you have a good idea does not mean others will automatically buy into doing it.

- Getting clarity out of chaos requires a leader to help others stop, breathe, think, and collaborate on a plan to follow.

- Remembering the names of those you meet is a great way to leave a positive impression and to let them know you care about who they are. Name association games can help.

- People best remember others who can make them smile and laugh. Never underestimate the power of a sense of humor.

- Life is a stage. We can learn a great deal about communication by understanding how actors do it.

- One of the best ways to improve our communication skills is having conversations with people like sales associates and food service waiters who are paid to talk to you.

- Focus on finding similarities and what you have in common with others. This is the fastest way to build rapport, even with adversarial people.

- Difficult people can be almost impossible to change. It is better to avoid them and release them as soon as possible. If you cannot replace them, you must remind them of your common interest to positively influence their behavior.

- Asking positive questions has no downside. It is the best way to learn, take an interest in, and influence others.

Chapter Six

Action 4. Educate Yourself

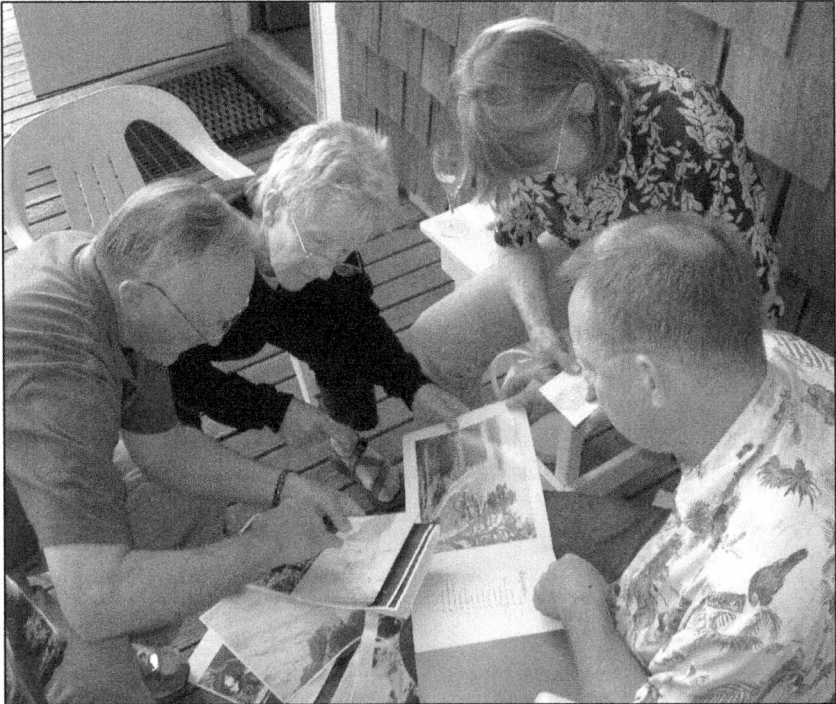

Captain Rick Rogers (right) and crew searching historical records on the hunt for a lost Spanish Galleon off the beach of Nehalem, Oregon.

Before my graduation from high school, a student counselor looked at me and looked down at my grades, then looked up at me and said, "Have you considered a career in Small Engine Repair?" Looking back, I guess I cannot blame him for suggesting that. It was not that I was ignorant, it was just at the time I didn't appreciate the importance of education and how what I was learning would equate to what I wanted to do in life.

When I was still in high school, I was told by a teacher that we would all need additional college or some form of secondary education. At the time I thought this was ridiculous. Living in Oregon, I was making good money in the timber industry and never gave much thought to going to college. Within two years the timber industry took a hit, closing the lumber mill where I was working. It was time to go to college.

I had to pay to take English and writing classes at a community college when I could have learned what I needed in high school. My point is as a young person, you have no idea of the opportunities you will have in your life and what education you will need to take advantage of them. I went on to put myself through college, getting an associate degree from a community college, then a bachelor's degree in Business Management from *Northwest Christian University*. I thought that might be the end of my education. It was only the beginning.

You Are Not done Learning

Think of it his way, you made it through high school. You now know just enough to be dangerous. If you graduated from high school in the United States, congratulations. Your education, while the most expensive, is ranked 24th in the world. (Source: 2020, *US News & World Report*, Best Countries for Education).

A bright young lady who is a friend of the family was top of her class valedictorian in an Oregon high school. When she returned to her home country of Germany, they required her to repeat her senior year. A U.S. educational ranking of 24 is disgraceful. Would you go to a restaurant or a movie ranked 24th? No. So why do we tolerate this from the most expensive education system in the world?

If you are one of the surprising large percentage of young adults who never completed high school, stop whatever you are doing right now. Drink an energy drink and find a way to get a high school diploma or at least a GED right now! There are many options to do this. On-line, through community colleges, and programs. Maybe from the school you dropped out of. Just do it and get it done as soon as possible.

Why is this so important? You will need to create a resume and stating you can watch TV and play video games will not inspire anyone to hire you. Not only do you need to list that you have a diploma or a GED, you also need to list what your other areas of learning or focus. Maybe a second language, computers, a sport - something to show you took initiative to be engaged and you have an interest in learning.

Then, there is college or trade school. This is just the next step to convince an employer that you can complete something else and this time it is more serious. You need to pay for it or at least get a loan for continuing your education in an area of focus of what you want to do.

If you are not sure what you want to do or major in, that is okay. As you proceed through this book we will go through this process in detail. No pressure, but if you choose wisely, you can pay off your education, have a happier life and an amazing career. If you choose poorly you will probably drop out, choose something else and be paying student loans off for years.

Choosing a College Major like Picking a Stock
Your education is kind of a big deal. Whether you have the money or are borrowing it, next to real estate, it is one of the biggest investments you will make. The good news is if you choose the right major and follow through, your education will pay for itself many times over. Trade school or Ivy League, the goal should be the same. Choose a major and make a plan to pay for it. Enjoy your time in college, but get it done as soon as possible. The sooner you do, the quicker you can become gainfully employed to pay off your student loans and get on with life. Going to school is fun - usually some the most memorable years of your life. But, getting on with your career and making money is even better.

When you pick a stock to invest in, you do so because you believe it will increase in value. You look at the long-term history of that career and talk with knowledgeable people on what the future prospects are. Practical questions to ask are how technology, the economy and political leaders could affect it. Your homework begins when you start to consider majors. Do your research and ask questions:

Are there special grants or loans for this major?
Is there a department student advisor I could talk with?
What are the job prospects like once I graduate?
How long does it take to get hired on the average?
How much can I expect to earn the first year?
How much can I make after five years?
What fringe benefits typically come with this career?
Do I have to relocate and if so, what are the best cities?
What would be the next step if I wanted to advance further?
Is getting an internship part of the program?
If so, do I find the placement, or do you help with that?

You cannot ask too many questions. Successful people don't guess about things.
They make decisions based upon more intel and not less. Do not take this too lightly.

Your career could last 30-40, or more, years. Long before my wife and I were married she was a single mother who needed to start a career. She wanted to work with other people, make good money, and have a flexible schedule. She decided to enroll in beauty school and become a hair stylist. It was an excellent and successful choice for her. Decades later she is still at it and many of her clients have become friends. It was a perfect selection for her that paid off well.

Working for Free Pays Big

When doing research on your career, one of the things you should be looking at is who you want to work for. What company, what city and how much are you going to make? This is important to have a goal established to be working with a path in your mind on how to get there. During your research, a question you should be asking is about interning or an apprenticeship with the company. Sure you want them to hire you for a full-paying gig. But what if you are not there yet? Maybe you need experience or to finish college first.

Ask for the internship. It is a win-win-win deal. You should be able to get college credit for it as well as get critical experience and contacts. The employer gets to see you working hard for them. During which time they will be evaluating you as a requirement for the internship, but also most importantly, they will determine if they should hire you when you are ready. Another huge advantage besides the training is that you should also be getting feedback on your work performance.

You Just can't get this type of real-world experience in college. When I was about 20, my first professional job was obtained through college. The owner of the company and I became friends and he hired me. This experience taught me more than I could have learned anywhere else. How to be professional, dress, travel, communicate, write, and work. I owe a lot to this man who gave a young kid a chance.

The college may have a placement plan for students to complete an internship requirement. Makes you look much more like a go-getter than if you find your own. You pick the company that you want to work for and tell them that in the process. You test drive them, and they test drive you. No big money commitments until you both know it makes sense that you work there.

If they say they do not have an official internship process, tell them you will help establish one. Ask them what things they would like to see done but they just do not have time for.

Every busy professional has a list of things they would like to do. Maybe new and exciting projects they do not have time for. But if an energetic and enthusiastic student approaches them, it might be just the right time to start off the perfect working relationship.

Being An Expert in Being An Expert

This line came from a U.S. Army Special Forces friend of mine. They would have a mission where they had to become an expert overnight a subject, location, or language they knew little about before. Maybe work undercover with the need to assume an identity of someone who is a specialist. He said they would spend the night researching the subjects and memorizing information from all sources possible. Not only did they do all that cramming in 8-12 hours, but it had to be accurate. You think a bad grade is tough? If they missed a detail, the mission could fail, and consequences could be life or death. If these guys can be experts overnight, you can do it within your own schedule.

College may not make you an expert. You will have to take the initiative to do that yourself. What most college professors are going to cover are the basics and generalized information, some of which will be outdated. I don't want to undervalue this, you need the basics before you can be a specialist. With the Internet, there is more information at your fingertips that any other time in history. This allows you to acquire data on any subject instantly. The problem is, however, anyone can post anything so how do you know it is correct? You need multiple sources from credible people and organizations.

It is interesting how many professionals you can meet, ask them a question and when you get just past the surface of the subject matter, they are clueless. I think to myself, wow, I cannot be the only one who has asked this question and they had no clue. They might try to redirect you to a website or something. This will not work for you. You will need to dig deep and learn everything you can about your chosen profession. I have done this on many topics and have enjoyed the process. Instead of looking at it as work, think of it as fun and inspiring to learn something new.

Podcast Make you Smarter

Successful people utilize down time with something educational or productive. Seems like we all have some time during the day where we are driving or traveling. Music is great but the same songs can get tiring. Listening to too much news can make you depressed.

Too much politics can make you agitated. The answer is podcasts. They can leave you inspired.

There is a podcast for about every subject you can think of. Typically, 30 to 60 minute programs with expert guests discussing the latest news and trends on the topic. Podcasts are free from an app provided or downloadable on your phone. They are great because they are produced in a way that make them entertaining and yet still educational. Before podcasts, it would be difficult to get this level of the very latest professional information instantly.

I listen to a few different kinds depending on the mood: business, political, inspirational, even topics like book publishing and stock investing. Podcasts are usually updated every day to once a week and I am convinced there is no better way to get caught up on any subject fast.

Trade Associations

One of the best sources of information for any industry are trade associations. Every type of business or industry has an association that provides the latest information, trends, and training. Join the association and absorb as much as you can. If you are a student, most associations have a lower-fee student membership program. They may even assist with a college scholarship.

Trade associations are great because they provide credibility while keeping you up on the latest news and information affecting the industry. This information is also vetted as coming from a credible source vs. just one guy's opinion from the Internet. These associations also provide reading and research materials through articles, experts, and bookstore sections.

One the best features of trade association is their conferences. It is great to meet up with a large group of like-minded professionals to learn and network. There are also lists of speakers providing the latest information. Listen to them, take notes, be on the cutting edge. Challenge yourself to learn so much you can do your own association presentation in the next year or two. I have done this and enjoyed the challenge. If I can do it, you probably can too.

YouTube It

Another great source for learning is *YouTube*. It is surprising how many how-to videos are on the site and it is a free. The only downside is that anyone can post anything. Do your homework and look at the comments, ratings, and number of views to make sure the information is credible.

It is a good idea to learn from multiple sources. If you are getting the same data from two or more sources, hopefully it can be trusted. I have used *YouTube* to learn everything from software to auto repair. I also have a few videos up there you can learn from yourself. At the end of the book I list a link to a keynote speech that inspired this book.

Social Proof

You will want to learn so much about your profession that you become an authority. It will not take as long as you think if you are willing to work hard at it. Get your degree, join a trade association, get professional certifications. From there you can present papers, give speeches, even write books. Doing so you makes you the expert or specialist that others come to for information. Trust me, I have done it, I have enjoyed speaking and writing books and I am no mental giant. Remember my high school guidance counselor suggested I fix small engines. I did not care what he said. I wanted success so bad I got serious about learning and doing what I could to support myself financially.

The first time I told people I wanted to write a book, they did not take me seriously. But I did anyway, it was about learning GPS navigation in 2001. Since then I've written five others and still counting. To be a writer, I needed to write. If you want to – (fill in the blank), then you need to do that. It does not matter what someone else thinks or what you tell yourself or others, you just need to learn how to do it, then do it. Think about when your friends go to a movie and they tell you it was so good, you should see it too. It could be the same with a good restaurant or a vacation place.

When your friends tell you something is good, and you see reviews that others have left, saying the same good things, you want to go too. Now you are ready to spend your money on the experience too because it feels like a safe bet. That is called *Social Proof*. You need that same notoriety in your career. You are the person who people are talking about and recommending to others.

That way if someone wants to hire you, they know you know what you are doing. You are the safe bet.

Leader of Leaders

As our world becomes more complicated, we soon find it will be impossible to know and be good at everything. Even though the information might be at our fingertips, we simply do not have time to become knowledgeable on every little thing we encounter. There are plenty of other people around to help us with that. To be successful, we must focus on what we are good at. We do that by allowing others to help us with what they are good at.

There was a time when I did my own taxes. I saved a little money but who knows, an accountant probably would have saved me more, even after paying them. As my financial situation became more complicated, it was no longer practical to do my own. I could have spent days learning about corporate tax law and possibly figured it out. But why? I have other business that demand my attention that make money. I do not need to know how to be an accountant, too. I am not good at it, I have no interest in it, and the stakes are too high if I mess something up. Under these circumstances, hiring someone else to do my taxes is the perfect thing to delegate.

A big part of being successful is not that you know everything. It's not that you should be really good at one or two things and be a specialist at one thing. What you need to do besides that is be resourceful. Have a cell phone full of useful contacts before you need them. Successful people get many things done fast. Not because they know and can do everything, it is because they know who to ask and hire to help them.

Having contacts in a variety of disciplines allows you to do two important things fast. First, is to get out of trouble is you have an issue. Second, is to get advice and take advantage of opportunities. It can also save you money in professional fees by being associates with these people. When you refer them to others, they could provide some services or a discount of their services to you.
Organizational development team specialist, John Chen calls this being the *Leader of Leaders*. Not only do you lead your own group, but you can facilitate cross-team collaboration coordinating operational information across many teams, groups, and organizations. Pay your dues until you can do this, and nothing will distinguish you more.

Remember, this book is not about being average and going with the flow. It is about knowing so much and being so resourceful that others demand your involvement to get the job done.

Time to Get Schooled

Consider what you can do now to increase your knowledge base and beef up that resume:

[ ] Get your high school diploma or GED
_____

[ ] Carefully consider your college major
_____

[ ] Carefully consider your college or trade school
_____

[ ] Take advantage of on-the-job training opportunities
_____

[ ] Interview and ideally intern with a specialist in your field
_____

[ ] Learn on-line from podcasts and videos
_____

[ ] Join and become active in a trade association
_____

[ ] Become an expert contributor for education in your field
_____

[ ] What else?
_____

The Least You Need to Know

- You are not done learning. Getting through high school and college are just the beginning.

- Pick your college major and career path carefully. It could either make you a fortune or bury you in student loans.

- Consider doing an internship. It will fast track your career and could get you a job if you impress the right people.
- Podcasts and videos are a great way to learn any topic you can think of fast. These are a great way to make commuting and other down time productive.

- Joining and getting active in a trade association is the best way to keep up with the very latest industry news and developments.

- Become so good that you experience 'Social Proof.' Others will hire you because you are recommended by your peers.

- Have the goal is being so well-known in your industry that you become a 'Leader of Leaders.' You know how to take advantage of opportunities and solve problems by knowing what other specialists to call who are already in your phone.

Chapter Seven

Action 3. Find Your Superpower

Shawn Cowles from Discovery Channel's Treasure Quest takes a break from Death Road driving to play with a centipede in Bolivia.

Superheros are kind of a big deal now. Most of the big budget movies are about them saving the earth or the universe. They get their powers from an alien race, genetic mutation, or a spider bite. What if I told you that you have superpowers, too? You might not be able to fly or punch through brick walls, but you can do something special that is unique to you. The origin of your superpower comes from a highest source possible, the Almighty Himself.

We all have some form of natural ability to do something or learn something really well. We also all have natural weaknesses - areas of our personality that need managed and improved on.

The trick is to foster our natural superhero abilities while keeping our natural weaker traits in check. If we can pull off that combination of personal management, we have something. A cape and mask that will only help us get stronger. And that is a positive thing because soon we will determine a life's mission to embark to use our power for good and not eeevil. I promise you, there will be times when we will need all the superpowers we can muster. No problem. We were built for this and will be training and preparing most of your lives. We've got this!

Before you leap from building to building, let's first define what your superpower is. For some of you, it is obvious. For others you have an idea, but it needs work. And, for some, you have no idea. Wherever you are at, it is all good. Now is the time to have a closer look at your talents and abilities to see what goes on your cape.

Let me provide an example by bragging on my kids. My son Eric, the oldest, is a natural musician. He can pick up nearly any instrument and completely rock it! Mikayla is my middle. She is smart, beautiful, can dance her heart out and is a born leader. When she is on a mission she does nothing but kick butt. Mikenzie, my youngest, is a stunning redhead. Smart, beautiful and extremely thoughtful. She is a natural at playing mediator and the voice of reason in chaotic times.

So, what are you good at? Maybe you are really good in one thing or have a few areas of talent. The following is a list of some obvious possibilities of traits and careers in alphabetical order. Have a look and put a check mark and notes besides the ones that are a fit for you.

Accounting
Actor
Agriculture
Artist
Athlete
Builder
Computers
Cooking
Courageous
Counselor
Creative
Designer
Doctor

Electronics
Engineer
Entertainer
Environmentalist
Financial
First Responder
Fixer
Hard Working
Healing Others
High Tech
Humorist
Inspirational
Legal
Leader
Making Money
Manager
Mechanic
Medical
Medicine
Military
Ministry
Model
Music
Nursing
Organizer
Outdoors
Parent
Peace Maker
Personable
Promoter
Protector
Public Service
Racing
Real Estate
Sales
Security
Service to Others

Singer
Speaker
Sports
Teacher
Therapist
Writer

What, No Superpower?

Okay, now you are just being bashful or selling yourself short. If you really think you have no God-given gifts, we can still work with that. You can always develop talents, but you need to work at it. That is if you at least have a positive attitude. This is critical. I would rather train someone with a positive attitude than a know-it-all with a bad attitude. Can you be likable? It is amazing what opportunities you can have if others like you. I am sure that I have gotten jobs and kept jobs over possibly more qualified people because I was able to make a friend and someone in charge liked me.

How about a sense of humor? My military friend told me that it seemed like the ability to make someone laugh was a determining factor if someone was promoted. Humor goes with being likeable. Do you attract people who enjoy being around you? If so, that means you can also communicate with others which is the first step in leading them.

If you are repelling people instead of attracting them, think about what subconscious issues could be at play. Could you be confrontational, self-absorbed, arrogant? Think about people who you are naturally drawn to and what traits they have. Could you learn from and adopt them? Every new encounter and conversation is a new beginning.

Here is the ultimate superpower - can you work hard? Ya, I know it's weird, but let's not overlook the obvious. The less talented can still beat the more talented by hustling and working harder. Even the best can get lazy and complacent. This is your opportunity to shine. You might be stuck in a job you do not like now, but as you move up the food chain, you will get better jobs.

Working hard is easier if you are doing something you like, and you can see progress. Like what you are doing means something and you can feel as if your life is getting better as you get ahead of things.

Show up tomorrow with a positive attitude, a smile and a lighthearted attitude and work your butt off. There is no a superpower better than that triple threat!

Fight Like a Superhero

I am using the term fight here because your life and career are that important. The level of success and money you can produce will determine how and where you will live and with whom you will live with. You may not like that. You might not think it fair. It may not be fair, but it does not really matter what we think, it is how life works. Would you drop $10 for a movie ticket to watch a superhero whine, complain, chicken out, and quit? I wouldn't either.

Think about how superheroes fight. Time to cape up and take a que from them:

Be the Alpha

Whether you are the one with the title or not, you are the one in charge. You do this by being completely aware of everything going on around you. You evaluate the task at hand and consider the most innovative and efficient way to get the job done. You are in complete self-control. Do not let your adversaries throw you off. You decide what kind of day you will have and choose to make it meaningful and productive. You take complete responsibility for the actions under your control or for what you can control. You stop, make a plan, and use positive communications to convey your goals and intentions. After a win, you smile, thank your people and kiss the girl (or guy).

Take the Hits

Life is not always sunshine and rainbows. Some days you will take hits. Everything will appear as if it is going wrong and you wished you stayed in bed. This is where mortals start to complain, and as another hit comes in, they think about giving up. Not you. You shake it off and pick yourself off the ground. You do not give up over a couple of punches. You smile knowing you are just getting started.

You are strong and know you can take much more than what they are dishing out. This is not your first or last fight, you have been here many times before. You put up your guard then bob and weave your head to not get hit again. Now when that spinning back kick comes in, it deflects off. You see an opening to strike back! No quitting or giving up. One, two shots in, direct hits, your opponent is now starting to stagger.

Momentum is now on your side. Gritting your teeth in determination, you fire back combinations of blows until you are the last one standing.

No Mortal is Going to Save Them
Superheroes do not slack because they think someone is going to rush in a save them. They know they are on their own. Other mortals simply do not have the power nor is it their job to do so. This is an important lesson we can learn from superheroes. What if we realized that no one is going to keep bailing us out after we do dumb stuff and make bad decisions? Maybe we could stop being a victim and learn to change our behavior.

Superheroes do not rely on any government agency to help them. They do not wait for other people, circumstances to change or to feel like doing something. They know they cannot borrow their way to prosperity and that their destiny is based upon their own actions. To save our own ass, we first need to get off it!

No Excuses
You don't hear superheroes say, "I could have saved the world if only…" or, "I could have stopped the villain of *Superman* hadn't got there first." No, they do not make excuses or blame someone else. Excuses and blaming doesn't make one appear smarter. It only projects weakness. When it is time for action, they take responsibility and act, fully knowing they are the only ones responsible for their success.

No Paralysis Through Analysis
When it is time to take action, they know there is not time to tell themselves they cannot do something. There is also no time to engage in multiple drawn-out, eyes rolling back in the head meetings. Superheroes utilize the *Management by Objectives* method where everything they do is to successfully complete the mission.

They do stop and make a plan first, but sometimes the planning has to take place while flying to the scene. Once the objective has been set and strategies on how to get there are determined, planning takes a back seat to action. Once engaged, the plan and strategies can be adjusted based upon the latest information and circumstances. The action continues however, as superheroes understand that movement and momentum win the day.

Unstoppable
Superheroes are unstoppable because they understand they cannot save the day half-way. They must keep working and fighting until the job is done. They do not stop to doubt themselves. They are mission-driven, persistent, and relentless. Nothing will stop them until the mission is complete. There will be time to rest, heal wounds and celebrate later. In the moment of the fight, concentration must remain focused on successfully completing the mission.

Look Good in Spandex
Superheroes are not sloppy, overweight, and drunk, not even *Ironman*. When the spandex goes on, they transform from a mild-mannered whoever to someone with superhuman abilities. The uniform provides a sense of pride and identity. Its symbols, badges and icons represent the unique authority and expertise of those who wear it.

When they wear it, they look and act like someone who should be in it like it is their destiny. That includes maintaining their physical appearance by eating healthy and staying in shape. Head high, back straight, chest out, shoulders back, stomach in, and shoes shined. Their uniforms are fitted, clean, color-coordinated and neatly pressed. Their unmistakable appearance gives them just the confidence they need when it is time to get the job done while bullets are bouncing off their chest.

Good Team Players
Superheroes complement each other's strengths. Although they have unique and typically specific talents and abilities, they know they cannot do it all. They are aware of their strengths and where they come from. They also understand the need to collaborate with others who are more knowledgeable or talented in a skill. If there is a shipping container of Kryptonite that needs to be recovered from the bottom of the ocean, *Superman* is smart enough to call *Aquaman*.

Life in general, especially fighting villains can be a complicated endeavor requiring a vast skillset. Most of us cannot be good at everything. There is just too much to have to know and do. This is true for us as well as superheroes, that is why they hand pick their team to overcome their personal differences and successfully get the job done. They understand the mission and that the overall goal is bigger than any one of their personalities or interests. They understand that individually, they can fail, but by standing and working together, they win.

Not Always About the Benjamins

Money is not everything. You do not see superheroes fighting for it. They know that if they are good at what they do, their financial needs will be adequately met, but getting rich is not their driving motivation. There is a bigger reward in doing the right thing and playing for a winning team. This is an *Intrinsic* reward that is much more valuable than anything you can buy or own.

Fight the Good Fight

Life is full of so many choices. Some are so obvious and clear while others are quite gray and convoluted. To be 'super' they must engage in superhero actions every day. Superheroes know what side they are playing for and they choose the good side every time. They do not compromise in this area. They do not say, we could switch teams to the dark side if it pays well enough and think they will not get caught. True, more money could be made in the short term with compromised values, but they know in the long run, it is just not worth it. They are thinking long term and big picture knowing if they go bad, even once, there whole persona is destroyed.

Superheroes also tend to run in packs where they are supported by others who share their good fight mission. If they are beaten down or tempted by their enemy, they find the support needed to get them back on their feet and in the fight. Following their mission keeps them on track. Decisions are easier to make if they are framed with, "Does this choice or action support the overall goal?" They wear their colors proudly. It feels good to do the right thing and playing on the right team. Superheroes understand that ultimately, they are not judged by their uniform, but by the action they take.

The Least You Need to Know

- Just about everyone has a God-given natural skill, intelligence, or something they are good at.

- If you believe you have no natural ability, then you must work extra hard with a positive attitude with the willingness to learn.

- Think about how Superheroes fight their battles. What can we learn from them? They take charge, no excuses, become unstoppable, and fight the good fight until they win.

Chapter Eight
Action 2. Give Thanks

Light coming through the stained-glass windows at my home church, Thurston Christian, in Springfield, Oregon.

Gratitude is the source of happiness in life. If you do not believe me, think of the ungrateful people you know. They are miserable. When you give thanks for what you have, even if you want more, you are still satisfied. Being humble and thankful immediately makes you feel better. It is a mindset that better connects with God. It reduces anxiety and depression generated through being obsessed with things that are out of reach or out of our control.

The ungrateful feel as if they never have enough and someone else owes them something. This is taking an entitlement or victim mentality. You do not have enough, not because you did not earn it, but because (fill in the blank). That is not to say there are no victims. Sure there are. There are millions of people around the world who have gotten a raw deal for some reason or another. But, how you react to your circumstance is a powerful thing.

In the year 2020, politicians pandering for votes flirt with the ideas of guaranteed income by just giving everyone money.

Getting free money might make us feel temporarily happy, but that is not the same as the internal satisfaction of earning with your own labor. Then, feeling grateful what you have received. Here is the unique thing about giving thanks – the more you give thanks, the more you must give thanks for. This is not a trick, but a reality in life.

By being thankful to those who have helped you, including the Almighty himself, you are in a humble position of gratefulness. Being thankful can allow more energy and creativeness to earn more and obtain even greater blessings. Give it a shot. It's free and I promise it will instantly make you feel better. Bow your head and say, "Heavenly Father, thank you for the gifts you have given me." Start to list them. There are more things to be grateful for than you might think: job, home, family, children, friends, health, possessions, opportunities, and blessings.

Nothing to Be Grateful For?

We in the United States and much of the western world have First World problems. We get upset and complain if we get a bad cup of coffee, shaky Internet service, or our plane is delayed. We have it so good, that we cannot remember what real problems are. Whatever you think your problems are, you do not have to look far to find someone else who would be perfectly willing to change places with you in a heartbeat. Stop whining and start listing what you must be thankful for.

Let us start with some basics. If you can eat and drink without getting sick you have something to be thankful for. If you can walk down a street without stepping in garbage and sewage, you have something to be thankful for. If you have the health to get out of bed in the morning and have an active day, you have something to be thankful for. If you have a house with a bed to get out of the morning, you have something to be thankful for. If you have work to do that will support you and your family, you have something to be thankful for. If you live in a free country with First and Second Amendments, you are luckier than about 95% of the rest of the world.

DNA Story

I could be on one of those DNA test kit commercials. My brother Kelly and I were adopted from separate families and raised by loving parents until they both passed. For a birthday present my wife purchased a DNA kit for me.

Within a month I found my mother's side of the family with five brothers and sisters. I got to meet and build a brief but amazing relationship with my beautiful and gracious biological mother before she passed the same year. The following year my father's side of the family with six sisters and one brother found me.

What an exciting journey it has been for me to meet all these brothers and sisters for the first time. The unique thing with DNA is that it is so exact and specific, no two creatures or humans on earth share the exact DNA. Only percentages of the exact characteristics are shared by those who are blood-related to each other.

Most scientists believed that life began in a primordial soup of organic molecules. After millions of years and a series of chemical reactions and mutations, these molecules became cells which eventually evolved into life. This primitive life creeped into the oceans and after more millions of years, eventually worked its way out to land to diversify to all the human and animal life forms we have today in and around our planet. This shaky, at best, theory was challenged with the discovery of DNA in 1953.

DNA is a molecule that works within our cells that storing and coding vast amounts of complex data. Each DNA molecule is composed of two chains that coil around each other to form a double helix carrying genetic instructions for the development, functioning, growth and reproduction of all forms of life. These DNA strains need to be programmed in exact sequences to define and create life. This sequencing is so exact, it is considered programmed. DNA molecules and their sequencing are so complex, there is no way they could have been naturally evolved by chance. Not any more than stacks of ones and zeros could marinate long enough to accidently convert into complex working computer software.

Due to this unique circumstance, some scientist use the term *Intelligent Designed*. Humanistic scientists can't come out and say that DNA was created by God, but at least they will admit it has to be created by an intelligent source verses somehow evolving by accident. So, if DNA tests can help us find our biological mother and father, is the fact that DNA was made by an intelligent source, proof there is a creator or a Heavenly Father? I am not here to preach, but to ask you to consider a larger prospective.

Purpose or Accident

I get it, a critical element of giving thanks requires having faith. Some believe in a God and some do not. I received my faith in a rather unusual way. Dad got HBO when we were kids and at the age of around eight, I snuck out to the living room and turned on TV and watched the *Exorcist*. After the movie, I was stunned and concluded that both good and evil do exist, and I was going to believe in and follow God. Since then, I have been a follower of Christ. I am not always good at it, but it is a long-lasting relationship that I work at, need, and appreciate every day.

You must consider the evidence for yourself. Look at creation and consider what you know and what you believe is the truth. Ultimately you must decide if we were all just accidental with no particular meaning or were we created by the Almighty for a purpose? In the Bible it says we were made in the image of God, and He has seen us before our bodies were formed and knows every hair on our head. It also says we were made for a purpose and to have an abundant life.

So, if you believe that you are child of a living God and a spark of faith has been ignited in your soul, now what? Will you think or act differently? How will you react to your newfound royalty? How will you spend your spiritual inheritance? Through my DNA test, I found my father's side of the family, the Scottish Clan *More*. I was excited to learn that my lineage goes back to include Sir Thomas More, an author, futurist, and knight. After standing up to King Henry VIII, he lost his head and the Catholic Church made him a martyr and saint. I was honored to learn this. How much more should we feel about our relationship and lineage to the creator of the universe?

Lightning and Grounding Rods

When lightning hits a building it would often explode and burn to the ground. That is because the structure was hit with so much electric energy there was nowhere for it to go. The lightning reacted like a bomb. This inspired the brilliant Benjamin Franklin to invent the lightning rod in 1752. With lightning rods mounted on the peak of a tall roof, and grounding rods into the ground, the energy from a lightning strike had a path to travel more safely into the ground. These simple metal rods saved buildings and lives.

Faith is like lightning and grounding rods. We constantly get subjected to life's storms.

Most could be a little gray skies and rain, others full blown thunder and lightning. We are going to take many direct hits in our life. Some type of conflict, drama, or terrible news. Without being grounded, even a minor hit can tear us apart. A major hit can have lasting negative effects for a lifetime.

If you are spiritually grounded, there is a path and a place for all of that negative energy to go. You can pass it through to God, ask Him to help you handle it. Ask for strength, wisdom, and courage to overcome any challenge that comes your way. I find that there is certainly no shortage of circumstances or situations to ask for help with.

You might ask why I might include this in a business and success advice book? This book is about balance and being successful in every aspect of your life. If you become wildly successful, you will still have problems. They just tend to cost you more money and energy to solve. If fact, the more successful you are, the more of a target you can have on you from others who are trying to get what you have, take advantage of you, or associate with you in the attempt to improve their status.

What is the point of working hard your whole life to acquire some money and notoriety, then not to able to enjoy it or pass it on to your family because you are spun out due to being overstressed, having mental health issues or taken by a terrible addiction? Giving thanks, faith and having a spiritual lightning and grounding rod will help keep you focused, content and on track. They will keep you grounded when a storm hits. And it will. Not only will you come out on the other side, but you will be stronger and thankful for the lesson.

Understand Your Value

We treat something to the level we perceive it. Cars have an engine and four rubber tires and any of them will get you from point A to point B. But we think of a *Honda Civic* differently than a *Porsche 911 Turbo*. All things being equal, we will take the keys to the *Porsche* because of how we value it. We will drive it more carefully although not any slower. We will be careful where it is parked, wash and wax it regularly, and make sure it gets the maintenance it needs. Repairs are expensive, and we want the classic to last decades.

If you were to feel this way about a car, why not feel even more strongly about yourself? You were made in God's own image. As beautiful as the lines are on a *911*, *Porsche* cannot make that claim.

When we value something, we take care of it. I am telling you - you are more valuable than you know. Everything about you is priceless. Nothing can help you rise faster than understanding your value. Not just potential, that is what you could do in the future. I am talking about your value, what you are worth right now. Once you acknowledge how valuable you are, you will think and act differently. You will treat others better as your respect increases for yourself. More importantly, you will also expect others to treat you better and with respect.

You will not allow others to take advantage of or use you. You will not let others be rude to you or try to manipulate or control you. You will not let others try to intimidate you or push you around. You will stand your ground and fight if you must. You will not give up your dignity, honor, ideals, or your virtue for the temporary approval of others. Knowing your value changes everything, you will walk a little taller as you lay the path for all the good things that are yet to come.

Straighten that crown or tiara, here is a breakdown of what makes you royalty:

Your Looks
You are stunning. Out of billions of people on this planet, no one else looks like you do. Have some pride and take care of how you look. Life should not be a freak show, have some class and style. The more you pay attention to your looks, the more your confidence will grow and the better you will feel about being in your own skin. We should not be obsessed about our looks; but, realize you will never look as good as you do right now.

Your Brain
You have been given a supercomputer that has more capacity then you can ever use. Protect your head so substances, chemicals or injuries will not leave lasting negative effects. Keep learning and fill up your brain with knowledge your entire life.

Your Dignity
Your dignity makes you who you are. It is your respect and humanity. Others could try to take it or abuse it, but you will not let them.

Dignity is a gift you give yourself. Because of your dignity, you will not let anyone take advantage of you or mistreat you. You will be a door mat or victim to no one. You will work hard to earn the respect of others. You will defend yourself and the honor of your friends and family. Regardless of the circumstances, others will know you will do the right thing.

Your Health
You have been given the miracle of the human body and everything it can do. The better you take care of it, the longer it will last. You would not take your favorite car out and beat it to death, use poor fuel, and not maintain it. Why do that to your own body? Treat your health as if you are going to live a hundred years. You just might.

Your Thoughts
What you think and tell yourself controls your mood, actions, health, and life. Positive input coming in results in positive actions. You decide what you want to do, then keep working at it every day until it is achieved. Garbage, self-doubt, and negativity coming in, what are the results going back out? Nothing good. Watch and listen to dark movies and music. No big surprise when you end up becoming depressed. You get where your thoughts lead you. Your perception of things is the strongest tool you have. Use it wisely.

Your Soul
Your soul is God-given and is your life's essence. Your energy and being lives on beyond your physical body. It is your supernatural connection to the creator as well as your moral compass. It will tell you clearly what is right, wrong, and which way to go. Protect and cherish it with all that you have. At the end of your life, your soul and your legacy will be what remains.

Your Family and Friends
These people are your greatest assets. They are the ones you love and who love and support you. That is why should never be abused by confusing them with business prospects. Do not try to sell them things or sell them out to a marketing company. Also, proceed with extreme caution when it comes to financial matters. If you owe them money, pay them back. Treat your friends and family well and they will be your biggest cheerleaders when you need them most.

Your Time
Everyone has the same amount of time in a 24-hour day. How is it that some get so much accomplished while others do nothing? Think of time like spending your money. You only have so much of it, so you must choose carefully what you spend it on. Usually there is not enough time to do everything we would like to.

We need to budget our time like we do our finances. So much goes to spending quality time with others, down time, even entertainment, while not forgetting the majority of the work week needs to be productive. Not just being busy by managing time to complete one accomplishment after another.

Five Stone Faith
My favorite story of the Bible is the fight between David and Goliath. David bought five stones for his sling in his battle with the giant Goliath. It was not because he was a bad shot, it was because Goliath had four other brothers. If you can live with that kind of faith, you will have nothing to fear. Carry five stones of faith with you. Nothing will stop you. Not only will you champion whatever challenge comes your way, but you will have four extra stones in your quiver for any other giants who dare rise up against you.

Timing is Everything
Seventy percent of those lucky enough to win a lottery go broke or bankrupt within a few short years. This is according to a study by *The National Endowment for Financial Education*. One of the main reasons cited was that once someone not used to having money, gets it, they lose the concept of reality. They buy dumb stuff and give lots of it away thinking it will last forever. Money does not last forever. In fact, just standard level living cost more than you think or plan for. This is got to be considered before buying high end homes, cars, and vacations.

I say timing is everything because understanding your timing and how everything can come together in life in an important part of being successful. When you get your windfall of cash it should be because you worked hard and earned it. By doing so, you have gained the maturity to understand the value of every dollar. This makes you think twice before letting all that money burn a hole through your pocket.

Wealthy people who keep their wealth typically do not waste it. They do not overpay for things or just give money away because someone talked them into it. When you understand the value of money, you will want to make more of it. Have income work for you by carefully investing in secure and reasonable ways, allowing you to increase your assets over time.

Not in fads or schemes, but in proven investments like real estate, precious metals and stocks, assets that continue to appreciate in the long term. Keeping and investing your money is critical for a successful life. Those who fail to learn how to manage money will end up working for an hourly wage until they practically drop dead. The bottom line is, if you are broke, you are a burden to others. Other people must bail you out of financial trouble or you will have to rely of the government to take care of you.

In contrast, if you do have money you can be a blessing to others. You can choose who you wish to help, ensure your children can go to college and support your favorite charities and church. Imagine the level of satisfaction you could have in the last half of your life with the ability of responsibly helping others with your wealth and knowledge.

We hunger for wealth and success. We see others who have material things within popular circles travel and enjoy life. We want that too. But to get there, we must understand so many aspects of life to reach that level of achievement. That includes knowing the value education, work, integrity, relationships, money, faith and being thankful. Once we learn, act, achieve and manage our blessings, I believe God can and will give you more blessings than you can ever imagine. But the Almighty works on His time and not ours. He knows that blessings provided before their correct time, will only be squandered like dust in the wind.

We need to be grounded and humble, giving thanks every day for what we have. Instead of feeling entitled, we are thankful for everything. At first, maybe you are thankful for simple things like your health and your dinner, then you find yourself giving thanks for bigger things and you are blessed in greater measure. Maybe that job you always wanted, the love of your life, a successful business, a new opportunity that can change your life! I want you to think about your legacy. As the saying goes, "You can't take it with you." Earn the money and enjoy blessing so many others before you die.

Love is a Verb

A good friend told me that once. It means that love requires action. It is great to tell someone that you love them. You should. It is even better to show them. God is not just found in church on Sunday. God uses people like us to do His work. And no, not just perfect people. There is no such thing. If you look at various Biblical examples you will see that He often uses dysfunctional people. Because people are not perfect, that means people like you and me.

If you want to know God, feel Him and have a relationship with the creator, there is no better way to do so than to do something that He would want you to do. That means love someone by being a loving person. That means taking time out of your schedule to do something for someone who could really use the support. Even if it means you get nothing in return.

There are no catches or expect something back from them. You do it because you want to do something that is the right thing to do. Like caring for someone who needs cared for. Be a friend to someone who could use a friend. Love someone who needs love, even if they are unlovable. There are lots of examples, and if you have a look in your own circle, there is no shortage of people who need a kind word and a lift up. Everyone needs love and encouragement, even the strongest among us.

What Can You Do to Enhance Your Faith?

Like going to a gym to get in shape, faith requires exercise and action to grow and get stronger.

[ ]   Pray and give thanks every day

_____

[ ]   Find others to talk to about your spiritual journey

_____

[ ]   Find a church to attend for weekly fellowship

_____

[ ]   Share your blessings with others

_____

The Least You Need to Know

- Grateful people are happy, satisfied people. Ungrateful people can take on a victim mentality and become miserable.

- The more you give thanks, the more you will have to give thanks for!

- If you feel like you have nothing to be grateful for, expand your view a little and you will find others who would feel lucky to have your problems instead of theirs.

- 'Programed' DNA strands all but proves that we were created by a higher power and not a primal soup accident. Time to decide what this means to you and how it will influence your life.

- Consider the grounding rod analogy to see how faith can protect you by being grounded through the next storm.

- Understand that everything about you is more valuable that you can ever imagine. Out of the billions of people on the planet, you are unique and come from the Creator of the Universe. Will you accept your royal heritage?

- God does not tend to give out blessings until we are in the correct mindset and have the maturity to appreciate and use them. Patience is needed as He works on His time, not ours.

Chapter Nine

Action 1. Find your Mission

Jack points the way with the Javier, Jeremy and off-camera Shawn, in Discovery Channel's Treasure Quest, Sacambaya Jungle, Bolivia.

Things are starting to get more interesting. We have gone through many details to get to this point. Are you ready to put it all together to complete the package? Finding your mission is the most important thing you will do in life. It changes everything. Instead of doing what others suggest or demand of you, you do what you were meant to do. This is what author Stephen Covey refers to as *Self Actualization*.

Lost and Found

When I was younger, I used to lead a four-wheel-drive volunteer search and rescue team in Lane County, Oregon. When someone was lost in the wilderness our team had a *mission* to go find them and bring them back safely. We did not use the terms; job, activity or task. No, when someone's life was at risk, the word we used was *mission*. The term mission has purpose and importance. Search and rescue teams need to operate based upon *Management Through Objectives*. This is because there are very limited resources of volunteer officers, vehicles, equipment, supplies, daylight, and time. When someone is lost, they are often confused, hungry, injured, wet and cold. The clock is ticking, and time is running out to successfully find and save them.

There is no time for endless planning, meetings, or busy work.

Leadership must make critical decisions in the moment to deploy the resources available based upon the intel them have at the time. Information available is often fluid, so changes are made, and new orders are carried out as the latest data is coming in. Leadership is about evaluating a flurry of incoming data, then quickly, but effectively evaluating and determining a plan. This is done to direct the needed, and usually limited resources available to be working in the field until the mission is successfully completed. The objective and consequences are clear. Success means to save someone's life; failure means to recover the deceased.

You are an induvial in a similar circumstance. Instead of finding yourself however, you need to develop yourself! You only have so much time and resources to achieve what you want to in life, then you are done. Goals, action, and results are critical. Are you here to goof off until you expire, or are you on your life's mission to leave your legacy?

Finding Your Triple Threat
Finding your mission in life will be the most difficult and important decision will you make. Some people are just lucky enough to know what they should be doing in life at an early age. Others struggle at this for decades. If you do not already know, think how great life would be if you knew what your life's mission is now? Think how much money and time you could save and how much happier you would be if you could finally focus and get down to business without years of drifting from one 'not quite right' endeavor to the next.

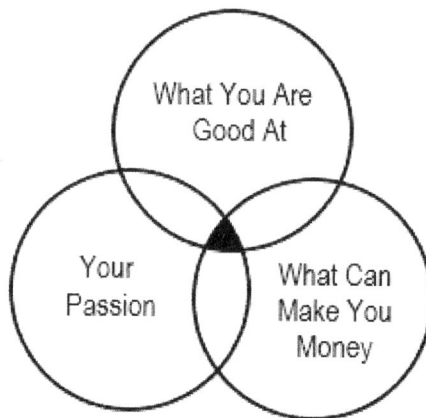

To know your life's mission, three important factors need to be in alignment.

What You Are Good At
This question gets back to, "What is your Superpower?" You might be good at a number of things. Think about a list of skills you are good at that you can plug into this equation. If you are stating that you do not yet have any marketable skills, you better show up with a positive personality and attitude and a truck load of enthusiasm.

Regardless of your age, you can always learn new skills. If you like what you are learning, it is surprising how short of time it can take to become good at something. Immerse yourself in learning and practicing until you are a champion. Here is your chance to write down your mad skills:

_____

Your Passion
Passion is the world's strongest emotion. It is what makes the world go around. It is the feeling that you must acquire something you deeply desire regardless of the cost. What you are passionate about? What gets your gears going and gets you out of bed on your day off?

What elements would be in a book, TV show or movie that would be so cool, you would instantly drop your last dollar for it. Can you do something related to that? If you can work with this emotion, it is no longer work. You no longer watch the clock or care what day it is. You are truly enthused to be in the game doing what you love. Write it down!

_____

What You Can Make Money At
I am adding money to the equation because unless you are lucky enough to be financially independent already, what you do has got to make money. Even if you have money now, it does not mean it will last forever. You cannot live your dream if you cannot pay the rent.

Life can be more expensive than you think. I know many times when I felt like I was getting ahead, something happened to relieve me of any extra money I thought I had. At this point, unfortunately, it seems that both persons in a couple must work, even for a modest lifestyle. Most of us will work for the majority of our lives. Pick something that pays enough money to do and live that way you want to. This is critical because poverty will suck the energy and fun right out of your life. What can you make money at and how much would you like to make?

_____

Think about these three factors carefully. No pressure, but this one of the most critical decisions of your life. If you cannot think of anything, you now a have a mission to find your mission. Remember, to be successful, you need to have all three. Or, you might be lucky enough to have a few options where you can successfully apply all three factors. Now it is the time to narrow it down so you can get focused.

What you are good at _____

What you are passionate about _____

What you can make money at _____

Now considering these three factors, what are the possibilities of your life's mission? Write down your possibilities:

_____
_____

Congratulations, this is serious progress! I have many interests, but it was easy for me to come up with possibilities that met all three criteria. I did discover I could not always make money at my endeavors. In fact, most of my passions cost me money. If you cannot make a reasonable living at something, it is an interest or hobby. For your primary mission, you need all three factors.

You Own the Mission

It is yours based upon your careful analysis. Write it down, sign and date it. Pin it up on the wall for you to see every day. It is yours and yours alone. This was not a casual decision on what you will 'try' next. This is your own mission based upon the three factors you carefully considered on what you are good at, what you are passionate about, and what you can make money at.

My oldest daughter is going to college to be a dental hygienist. At a business conference, I randomly ran into a table of dental hygienists who were just finishing their association conference while ours was beginning.
I told them about my daughter wanting to join their ranks, and one of the ladies gave me her ID name badge for their professional dental association. I wrote my daughter's name in the card and gave it to her. Now she had something tangible to see her name attached to the profession.

This is critical because you must see yourself do the mission and believe in it with all your heart before you expel the energy needed to reach your goal.

I asked my daughter to pin this name tag up and remember it. When she is buried in homework, wants to give up or if someone is trying to pull her off-course, she needs to look at her name on the tag and believe she belongs there! It is her mission. We all need to be able to visually see ourselves in our mission and believe it with everything we've got.

Your mission is your unique dream and desire. Except you are not just going to dream about it, you are going to do it because it has so much purpose and value. Your mission is your intellectual property. It is what a business would file a patent or trademark for. It is your magic beans, your secret sauce. It is what gives you and your brand great value. You need to protect it as such. It is worth more than gold because it is your happiness, purpose, future, and legacy!

No one is more responsible for you to reach it than you. Not your parents, your teacher, or your spouse. Only you. If you do not care, no one else will either. If you get dragged off-course by some other distraction, it is no one else's fault but yours! If someone says, do not complete your mission because I have a better offer, you can consider it, but at the end of the day, you must be true to yourself.

Your brother-in-law wants you to help him sell emu meat futures. Is that a better deal? Is that your original mission? If so, great you are on your way. If not, tell him no thanks, and stay on track for your own mission no matter what! Everyone has their own purpose and mission. They will pull you off track because they see a smart enterprising person in you.

Of course, they would like your help in completing their mission. He needs to build his own team and you will also. If your brother-in-law is good at sales, he might just convince you that emu meat is the wave of the future and you are foolish not to get on the ground floor. I am guessing you did not grow up dreaming about emus.
You probably did not even consider them as a career possibility, but if you do not wake up in the morning springing out of the bed with the passion of all that is emu, better stick with your own mission.

You own your mission, meaning you in are in control of your own destiny. No blaming anyone else and no excuses. If you fail and must sell emu meat futures, that is on you. If you waste seven years of your life messing with emus, instead of completing your own mission, that is also on you. If you succeed to spend the rest of your life satisfied knowing you are doing what you are supposed to do, well raise your glass and smile. Cheers. That was all you. Enjoy your reward!

I want you to remember this, so I am really hammering it home. If you follow the Goldfish Actions, you will distinguish yourself and you will find yourself in the greatest demand of your life. I am not exaggerating - I promise you this. Others will see you looking good and dialed in, smart, motivated, and following your dreams. Not a big surprise if they will want you to help them with their dreams too. They will want you to:

> Be your friend
> Attach themselves to you
> Date you, be your lover
> Possibly marry you
> Ask you to join their team
> Hire you
> Ask you to manage their business
> Offer you ideas and business proposals

Without some discipline, this could all be very overwhelming as others attempt to persuade you, even seduce you, to their own interests. Go back to your own mission. Does it fit? If not, smile and keep moving to stay on your own track.

Plan B

What if you have a good job already? If you do, that is great. My father enjoyed his career with the same company for 35 years, but that type of longevity does not seem to be as prevalent as it used to be. There have been times where I thought I was working my 'forever' job, then something happened. I had bosses get sick and die and run off in scandal. Agencies change leadership, companies change ownership, political and market winds can change in a moment.

No one knows what could happen next. At the time of this writing it is the middle of 2020 which is the poster child for years of chaos and change. Always have a Plan B. Never get caught off-guard.

Consider what you will do if your current career or employer is somehow jeopardized. Don't ever allow your current situation to be your only option.

Sometimes you will find yourself in a no-win situation and it is time to take action instead of becoming a victim of circumstance. I have been on sinking ships and was happy to jump off before the bilge and rats reached the deck. I have no interest in going down with a sinking, losing ship, and you should not either. Always be thinking of a Plan B no matter how good things are going now.

Owning the Mission When You Do Not Own the Agency or Company

Many of us will work for an agency or company that we will never have physical ownership of. Most career paths fall into this category and they offer unique challenges and opportunities. While many of us would like to own our own companies, it is not as easy or romantic as it is thought to be. As a business owner, much of the time is spent doing a variety of administrative tasks leaving little time to do the work you originally got into the business to do. You must start somewhere, and it is usually for someone else. Even if you do not own the business, you still need to own your job.

Being an employee has its advantages in that you are typically working 40-50 hours a week where you can focus on being very good at your job and still have enough hours left in the week to enjoy your life. This is helpful to understand because as a business owner, there may be an additional 10-20 per week to cover the many behind-the-scenes tasks that employees do not have to deal with.

The following is an example of three different categories of how one could be an employee for an agency or company as well as the possible opportunities and challenges that come with each:

Public Service and Safety
Police, fire, EMT, courts, utility, city, county, and state government:

Attracts a variety of employees both motivated and not.
Everyone typically makes the same amount of money although typically good pay, retirement, and benefit packages.
Difficult for raises and bonuses to be used as an incentive.
Highest levels of regulation, bureaucracy, and politics.

Most likely union-based that will have an effect on management and wage structure.

Large Organizations
Education, universities, hospitals, airports, Fortune 500 companies, service, manufacturing, state agencies, federal agencies, military:

Can attract more competitive employees.
May start off making base salary, but possibly more opportunities to advance.
Greater possibility to negotiate higher wages.
High levels of regulation, bureaucracy, and politics.
Multiple management layers can allow the best opportunity for advancement.

Private Companies and Firms
Small businesses, franchises, construction, retail, engineering, legal, insurance, lending, real estate, investment, medical offices:

Can attract the most competitive employees.
Smaller companies may be limited on how much they can pay.
Greater wages tied to incentive work and commissions.
With smaller staff sizes, understanding how to negotiate regulation, bureaucracy, and politics will be beneficial .
Simpler management structure may provide less opportunities for advancement.
May provide an opportunity to take over or purchase the operation from the owner, especially if you can help them retire.

As a business owner, they must take complete ownership of every aspect of their business. If they do not, their business will quickly fail. But what about as an employee? Can you still take ownership of the job even if you do not physically own anything about it?

The answer is yes! Even as an employee you should have an ownership mindset of your work. You should be trained to think and work that way, but even if you are not, take the initiative to do it anyway. This is how you are going to distinguish yourself and move up the food chain.

Take Responsibility for Everything Within Your Control
If a business owner sees an issue, they cannot say, "It's not my problem, let someone else worry about it."

If they did think that way, they would not be in business very long. I want you to think like a good businessperson to become one. No passing the buck.

If you see a tangible issue within your control, you own it! Deal with it, fix it, make it better. If it is not in your control, then you need to bring it to a manager's attention. If possible, help then solve the issue. Help build a company culture through example of taking responsibility and finding solutions.

Communicate Up and Down the Chain of Command
You might think it is enjoyable to communicate down the chain of command. You get to boss people the tell them what to do.
It is not as easy as it may seem. In fact, if someone under you does not understand or carry out a directive, that is your fault not theirs!

A leader must communicate in a way that is simple and direct, then ask questions if necessary, to ensure those below them understand two things. First, what is the mission? Second, what role they play in completing it? More specifically, what do they need to do now to make it happen. Letting them in on the bigger picture of the mission is critical because if there is any confusion, they know what the desired outcome is of the organization. You are telling them what and why.

Here is the harder part, you must also efficiently communicate up the chain of command. Often this is done by endless reports and paperwork, but it should be verbal as well. Leaders or want-to-be-leaders must have the courage to address and openly communicate with those above them. When you get told what to do, you need to ask questions to clarify if necessary. If something does not make sense, you need to ask why. Ask them to give you the bigger picture so you can understand what you are being asked to do.

This is critical because you can't effectively pass down directives from above and expect those under you to help you carry them out if you do not believe in or understand the mission. Be bold enough to ask why. This is so important.
Very little else will have the impact on your success than the ability to communicate with those both above you and below you on the management chain.

93

Encourage, Thank and Train Others

One of the first steps in becoming a leader is being so good at your job you are asked to train others. This is a great opportunity because those new people who you are training are looking up to you as an authority. You can train them right the first time before bad habits are learned or set in. As they learn, you encourage them and thank them when they go above the beyond what is expected. Chances are the more you encourage and thank them, the harder they will work and go above and beyond.

As they learn, share with them the tips and tricks that work out best for you and other seasoned people to reduce the learning and frustration curve. Guide them but also let them come up with ideas and solutions on their own. This is what builds the confidence needed for them to take the next level step in learning the business.

As the years go by, it is very satisfying to see the new person you trained become a leader and watch them thrive and train others. It will make you proud to see your influence being passed down to new people as part of your legacy.

Work With Others to Make and Execute Operational Plans

When you get a group together, even an experienced group, it tends to look like an unorganized cluster. Without direct leadership, communication is poor, and people are running off in different directions trying to figure out what to do and how to do it. The trick is to catch them before they all run off to do their own thing.

When everyone gets together, and the mission is announced, then it is time to stop and make a plan. Others will appreciate this because running in circles and duplicating work is no fun. Being confused, frustrated, and looking for something to do to appear busy is not fun either. People want to feel productive and know what they are doing will directly contribute to the cause. This is why they appreciate good leadership.

Depending on your administrative authority, it might be something you decide, direct and delegate. "Your team does this, and your team does that. Let me know if you have any questions and I will meet you there." If you are one of the line staff with no official authority, you can still do this, it just requires more diplomacy. "Why don't we look at some possibilities to determine the best way to get this done?

How about if our team does this, and your team does that, and we meet at..." Learn to recognize when people seem confused and not sure what to do. It is more often than we would like to admit. Help them and guide them with structure and ideas. They will recognize you as a leader regardless if you have the title or not.

Encourage Working in Teams

There is a huge difference in people that operate within Work Groups and those who operate in an effective High-Performance Teams. The difference is staggering so you will want to work in and eventually lead high-performance teams. If your employer does not already, you will want to encourage a team structure. If there is no official team structure, you can still get your rag-tag co-workers to possibly overcome their personal interests and differences to act like a motivated team.

Work groups tend to have poor leadership, so the members are off doing their own thing with little or no communication. Without good communication, there is little sharing of best practices and training is lacking. Due to a lack of clarity of the common mission, members tend to be very competitive with each other. There is little assisting others or collaborating, but plenty of gossip and backstabbing. Morale is dirt-low. Many call in sick and the ones that do show up and hold it together have already sent off resumes to work somewhere else.

You want to work in an environment that is opposite of this mess. The basis of a high-performance team is trust and communication. Regardless of the type of team it is, without trust and communication you have a dysfunctional work group. As a leader, with an official title or not, you can foster a work environment of trust and communication. With this critical attribute and an ongoing focus on completing the mission, you can get people from all walks a life to come together to accomplish great things.

The next level of efficient teamwork is you establishing Cross-Team Collaboration. This is a fancy way of saying that various teams within the same agency or company communicate with each other.
If there is no official protocol or network of communication, you can be that person who is in contact with other leaders to convey information needed to ensure all teams have what they need to work effectively.

Encourage Communication, Collaboration, and Innovation
Once you are working within a team structure and communication is flowing, be prepared for magic to happen. When co-workers are encouraged to communicate and freely share ideas, they will, and innovation takes place.

Someone has a good idea and shares it with the team. Someone else considers the idea and thinks of a way to make it even better. The ideas are expanded on further with exciting enthusiasm as innovation runs wild. Obviously not every idea is good or will be implemented, but with collaboration and innovation, new ideas will be implemented that will be better that than you previously imagined.

With trust, communication, and encouragement your team and company can enjoy this innovative free flow of ideas. Most employees know how to do something better, safer, and less expensive, but they will not say anything because they are not asked. We all want to contribute to a cause we can believe in and be recognized publicly for our ideas and contributions. We do not want to take the risk of an idea if it will be ridiculed or stolen as the boss's idea.

Give the credit to others when they provide ideas and contribution. If you do, it will be no surprise that your team will be thinking every day, "How can we do this job even better?" Not all ideas are usable, but some will. Ideals you have not thought of. Ideas so good, that you and your team will want to implement them. Give them the credit and thank them for their innovation. You can get credit for leading a team whose positive communication and innovation will run circles around the competition.

Keep it Simple
Many people struggle with their plans and missions their entire life without doing much of anything because what they want to do is too complicated. Good ideas do not have to be complex. Break your project down to simple visually achievable goals and work in phases.

For example, phase one is planning. Once everything is planned out on paper, then move to phase two. This involves creating the structure to make it happen like logistics, funding, and people.
Phase three is doing. Putting the plan in action to make it happen. Phase four is making improvements to keep it sustainable and help it grow.

Looking at the big picture can be overwhelming. Break it down into bites you can achieve. Every time you reach a goal it encourages you and others to keep going until the next marker in line is complete. Most projects in life are complicated, yours can be too. Just take on more complex issues in stages. Let your airplane fly first, then add on more features once you have taken off and landed a few times.

Not Everyone is Going to Be a Fan

The advice I am giving you is counterintuitive to what a typical employee might do. I know what some of you are thinking - You are asking me to do all of this? Things that most others will never do? What if I just want to work and get a check to enjoy my weekend? Remember, you do not have to do anything.

You do not need to read this book if you are only striving to achieve mediocracy. This book is not about how to follow the masses down the multi-lane highway of least resistance. It is about distinguishing yourself. That means you are going to do what most others will not do.

Be aware that some will admire you. You will inspire them and they will become your cheerleaders. They will be excited about your growth, success, and will want to work with you. They will friend you on social media and send you notes years later telling you what a positive influence you had on their lives.

Also be aware that others will resent you. They will think you are trying to make them look bad. If this is the case, they look bad already, but that will not stop them from throwing you under the bus or sabotaging your efforts. They may even try to get you fired. Politics at work can get ugly and it is nearly everywhere. Being a distinguished leader means learning how to deal with negative politics. Learn to get yourself up and out of the mud. Better yet, don't get in the mud in the first place.

You must stand up for yourself, not be bullied and even be prepared to fight. This will challenge communication and leadership abilities. If you are getting into a possible entanglement, let those you answer to know in a clear and precise way.
Write the facts down to keep a written record of the circumstances in the event you have defend yourself legally or physically.

Be strong, be focused, be professional and carry on.

97

The idea of this book is to help you rise above any drama to live your fullest life as soon as possible. Living well and helping others is the best revenge. Let your positive achievements and actions speak for themselves. I am telling you, it is worth it.

Want to Get High?

Alcohol, pot and drug sales are through the roof. As recent events have made life more uncertain, and people become more anxious, they turn to substances for an escape. The problem with these substances, however, is that they may make you feel good temporarily, but there are negative side effects like bad hangovers as the alcohol and drugs wear off and reality comes creeping back.

What if I told you that it is possible to get really high? A euphoric feeling that does not go away and no hangover. When you think about what you are doing and the achievements in your life, all you can do is smile. It is possible and obtainable. There is no better feeling than doing what you were meant to do by pursuing your mission.

It does not mean that you are rich and life is perfect. But even small victories from your hard work can make you higher than any substance you can take. The only side effect is that success feels so good, you want to work even harder to achieve more. More victories are reached, and the 'high' cycle repeats itself. Believe me, it is awesome. Sometimes I just grin like an idiot and give thanks I am so blessed. Try it for yourself. What do you have to lose?

The Least You Need to Know

- One of the most important decisions of your life is what mission you will pursue.

- Unless you are independently wealthy with no chance of running out of money, your mission must include all three factors: What is your passion? What you are good? And what you can make money? You cannot live your dream if you cannot pay the rent.

- Your mission is unique to you alone. It is your magic beans and intellectual property that gives you great value. Hold it close and treat it like gold.

- Even if you already have a great career, it is smart to have a Plan B. Events and circumstances can happen to make forever jobs disappear in a flash. Moving to Plan B gets you back in the game faster.

- Learn to think and act like an effective leader and business owner. If you see something, a problem or opportunity within your power, you own it! If it is not within your realm, tell someone above you.

- Even if you do not own the company or lead the agency you should still take ownership of your job. Nothing will distinguish you like influencing, encouraging, and leading others regardless if you have a title or not.

- Getting others to work within teams while utilizing trust, positive communication and innovation will give you an incredible advantage over any competition. There is no better way to test and showcase your leadership ability. These skills will serve you well regardless of what you do throughout your career.

- Understand that most others will not expel the energy or effort to do anything close to what I am asking you to do. Some will appreciate you, others will resent you.

- The idea is for you to be as successful as you want to be to live your best life as soon as possible.

- Remember my question about if you want to get high. There is no better feeling than reaching Self-Actualization by doing exactly what you were meant to do. This is a natural high that cannot be beat. And no hangover.

Chapter Ten
Life is a Race

No fear, no excuses, no blaming. Desert race team 6147 crosses the 2019 Vegas to Reno desert race finish line on three tires.

I know you thought life was a journey, well I am calling it a race. There is no urgency in going on a journey. You get there when you get there with no time schedule or specific direction. That is how most of us live our lives. We just cruise along until one day we wake up and realize we are now older and have not accomplished what we wanted to do.

Time goes by so quickly, do not waste your years! There is just so much to do and experience. Put a great value on your time and let me help you get into the race. You may have noticed that I enjoy desert racing. Come along with me for a desert race analogy to help bring all the Goldfish Principles together.

Dream Big Goals
When I was a kid, I built an off-road go-kart and raced BMX bikes. I had always dreamed about racing across the desert at full speed in a famous race like the *Mexican Baja 1000*. Looking at this dream on paper, there was nothing that made sense about it.

It requires stacks of stupid money and countless hours preparing a race buggy or truck. It also requires a motivated crew who is as equally as crazy, willing to use up their vacation time to risk their lives in a foreign country to help.

Nothing about it is a good idea except I require high levels of adrenaline. Desert racing fits the bill as the most exciting and challenging sport I can think of. I have given up on this dream before and instantly became depressed. The thing is with dreams, whether we do them or not, we still need them. It is part of what gets us out of bed and keeps us going. Go pro, dream something big. Be careful, with enough focus and tenacity, that dream might come true.

Reach Visually Obtainable Goals

The Baja 1000 desert race is 1,000 miles (1,609 Km), stretching from one end of the Mexico's Baja peninsula to the other. This is the most demanding race in the world on the drivers, crews, and machines. Despite everyone's best efforts, only half will reach the finish line.

If we zoom out too far to look at the big picture, our goal can look very overwhelming. In our example, we are asking the team to race 1,000 off-road miles across Baja where only half of the teams finish. Why bother? But what if we break down the race in legs? Instead of looking at 1,000 miles, we look at 80 miles to the first checkpoint. Wow, that sounds a great deal easier. Once we make it to the first checkpoint, now we can focus on making it to the next checkpoint. We do have the big picture in mind, that is our mission, but we focus on the individual legs that get us there.

Fortunately, life and life events are broken up in sections this way, grades, laps, levels, and degrees. We work to advance or graduate from one level to the next higher one. It is so much easier for us to focus on the next challenge along the way instead of every aspect of life at once. This is because it is easier to keep going by reaching visually obtainable goals. We are no longer asking ourselves to do the impossible, we just need to finish the current grade, job, challenge - whatever we are doing. When we can see our progress, it is inspiring. We work harder, fight longer until the section is marked off our list. We take our victory and what we have learned to move on to the next.

Goldfish Principles Go to Baja

Consider this idea with the seven Goldfish Principles. Each principle is a leg of your life's race. They do not need to be in order as I listed them, and you can do multiple at the same time. The point is that you pursue each one as a visually obtainable goal. Let us look at this idea in the desert racing analogy. Each principle is in its own unique order to match the specific application of my off-road racing story.

The Mission

We start with the mission: We are going to enter, race and attempt to finish the Baja 1000. To do so we will create a race team of a dozen handpicked members and acquire a race truck that will qualify within a race class for the event. The team will work, practice, and play together until they have the rapport and skillsets needed to go pro.

Time To Learn

We need to learn all we can about the race and all the logistics we will need to cover. We will need to support the race crew and vehicles from the start line in Ensenada to the finish line in La Paz. This includes lodging, fuel, food, drinks, as well as any parts or tires needed. Every team member will learn everything they need to know to work out any logistics necessary to do their job effectively.

Build the Brand

The race team gets branded. A team name, logo, and color scheme. Drivers and co-drivers get matching suits and teammates get matching shirts. T-shirts and stickers are available for fans and crew and make great give-a-ways. We also establish social media pages so fans can follow our adventure as well as track the truck in real time during the race. We will stream photos and videos as well as feature our team members and race sponsors.

Our high-profile branding will help us get additional media attention such as increased magazine and television coverage that will help us attract higher paying sponsors for the following race seasons.

Communication

To be successful in this adventure, we know that our communication game must be perfect. The first thing we have is a team mission that everyone is clear on. This conveys our team's purpose, goals, and the intent from leadership. This is important so when teammates need to make decisions in the field, they do so based upon the team mission.

We have two bilingual persons to cover the Spanish language while on ground. For the race, the truck and the chase support vehicles are all equipped with VHF radios programmed to the same channels. This allows us to communicate with race officials, emergency personnel and a channel for inter-team communication.

Satellite phones provide a backup. Satellite phone service also provides a tracking feature through GPS software so we can see the race truck and support vehicles live on the moving satellite GPS map. This allows a rescue or a repair to take place as soon as possible. Having two dependable ways to communicate and GPS location information takes the guesswork out of what is going on and gives us the confidence that we can resolve most problems to keep the truck and team moving to the finish line.

Using Our Superpowers
When the race team is created it is done so with handpicked people that each have their own superpower. The best two drivers, drive. The best navigators and radio operators, navigate and communicate as co-drivers. The support crew is made up of people who are motivated to fix things and get things done under any adverse circumstance.

These people who are selected, accept the mission and compliment the team. More importantly their talents and abilities make the team stronger as a whole. This means the team and the mission take priority over any one individual. It makes us competitive with all our collective talent giving us a real chance of making our goal happen.

Don't Fall Into Traps
Once the race is on, we are confident we can finish if we do not fall into any traps. No crashing, no rolling over or pushing drivers or machine over the breaking point. Flat tires and minor repairs are something we expect and can deal with. What we need to avoid is any major problems. Serious damage or engine failure will stop our valent effort dead in its tracks.

🏁 *Race Day!* 🏁

After all the hard work, preparation and getting the team together, it is finally race day.

We wake up early with the sunrise over the Mexican city of Ensenada. Two chase trucks take off early to position themselves at checkpoint two and three. The race truck rumbles through the staging area. Spectators line the dirt race road leading south out of town.

After waiting in a line of trucks in the same race class, one-by-one they get the checkered flag and disappear into a cloud of dust. Finally, it is our turn to approach the start line. The officials give us the thumbs up, start the timer and drop the checkered flag. Our engine roars to life as we power down a dirt road lined with sponsors' flags and cheering fans that include the locals and race teams and fans from around the world.

The engine is revving, blood is pumping, and the dirt is turning into a stream of dust behind spinning off-road tires. The first of two drivers attempt to calm the nerves to keep the truck moving fast but under control. Hyper aware, the rhythm sets in balancing speed and driving finesse. The driver and co-driver remember to focus on obtainable, visual goals. From the start, 80 miles to the first checkpoint, now only 71 miles to go.

The first checkpoint is now visible through the dust. We passed one truck in our class and are making good time. Our chase crew have arrived before us and are holding up a team sign. Driver and co-driver let out a sigh of relief to see them and get rewarded with bottled ice water as the truck gets a quick look over.

Two chase trucks are leapfrogging to each checkpoint to be ready for the race truck when it arrives. When the chase trucks make contact on the public roads, it turns into a competitive drag race. All in fun, but this puts our race effort in jeopardy as one of the race officials warned our crew chief for our chase truck to slow down. One of our trucks was seen nearly sliding off a corner on a public road taken at too high of speed. The crew chief radios into the truck, tells them to switch to a private channel to inform them to slow down and drive more careful.

Having one of the support vehicles in an accident or the team disqualified would make the driver feel terrible, but most importantly it would jeopardize our racing effort. The crew chief tells the drivers to use their competitive energy to help compete against the other teams and not compete against each other.

The race is going smoother than expected as we are moving from checkpoint to checkpoint.

Our chase crews meet us at each point ready to provide tires, fuel, and repairs. We are ahead of schedule and the race truck as well as the crew are performing like a well-rehearsed orchestra. This race is getting very exciting because we are doing so well. Electricity is in the air as the team works even harder to ensure we get a finish line checkered flag tomorrow morning.

We are now almost halfway through the 1,000-mile sprint. The sun is setting into the beautiful Baja Pacific Ocean and the mechanic tests the banks of lights and the electrical system to ensure the driver and co-driver can see through the night.

Everyone now, already tired, must step up to be hyper-vigilant. With vision reduced, the driver needs make sure he operates the truck as carefully as possible while still maintaining a high-enough speed. Yes, he could push the truck faster, but speed must be balanced with survivability.

The co-driver needs to make sure he is taking the right course and ensure they are on track to the next checkpoint. At this point, some have taken or moved the course markers and one dirt road looks like any other, especially at night. He also needs to use excellent communication radio skills to direct the chase crews to arrive at the checkpoints prior to the race truck.

The chase and support crews need to be moving quick and ready for anything. Driving at night in Baja is an adventure all in its own. One of the other chase trucks hit a rancher's steer in the middle of the road causing damage, injury, and a legal entanglement. Raging adrenaline needs to be balanced with awareness and effective thinking. Not always easy considering some of the crew will be up 30 or more hours by the time the race is complete.

They need to follow the GPS instructions to locate and arrive at each checkpoint prior to the race truck pulling in. Their eyes need to scan the truck carefully, looking for anything loose, broken or leaking. So far so good, dumping fuel, changing tires, and tightening some loose bolts, the truck is doing well despite losing a fender and part of the front bumper to a boulder.

The second driver of the co-driver team takes over around midnight to finish the last half of the race.

A truck that we already passed, caught up with us and left the pits before us. Stress is now even higher, but the engine still sounds great and the clock is ticking. The new driving crew needs to shake off their nerves and settle into their own rhythm to get the truck moving at a fast and steady pace. Within five miles the driver sees the competitor truck ahead of them and makes the move to pass. Dust is thick, visibility is zero. The driver overshoots a turn, slamming into a ditch.

The impact was so violent, the truck's electronics shut off, killing the engine. The drivers, shaken and choking on dust, only hope no one slams into their truck in the darkness. With the electronics out, there is no way to call for help. "We are 4 miles north of the checkpoint at Bahia de Los Angeles. We are losing power and sending you our location!" The engine stalls and the electronics go dark.

The drivers find the satellite phone and flashlights and go to work immediately. One chase truck is already at that checkpoint and the other is moving in fast looking for a route to intercept the race truck on the course. The drivers remove the hood to see a smoking alternator. This is most likely the problem and the co-driver gets on the satellite phone to alert the team.

One chase truck is directed to meet the race truck and the second is to remain at the checkpoint to find an alternator. The checkpoint has hundreds of race team crews and local spectators in a large party atmosphere. Many hanging around a large bonfire watching the racers come through with cheers.

With the race truck's lights off, it's a hazard as other race cars could hit it. The drivers wave flashlights at oncoming race traffic to avoid a collision A flicker of lights off in the distance is our chase truck coming in fast. The chase crew at the checkpoint is frantically trying to find a replacement alternator. The drivers text photos of the burned one in the truck as they remove it to help them find a match one.

The two guys in the Bahia de Los Angeles pits go from pit crew to pit crew, but are striking out. One of the local teams say they have one that will bolt up, but it is in their truck. A quick comparison to the photos texted through the sat phone confirms it looks like a fit. The strangers are willing to sell us their alternator. The guys collect their cash, throw in some t-shirts and stickers to finalize the trade.

The guys then drive out to the race truck to install the new part. After some minor modifications, the alternator is on, but the battery is too dead to start. After a jump start and final system checks the motor is running and the electronics are powered back on. Things are looking up, and the skinny pedal is down to make up 45 minutes of lost time just to regain their original position.

The sun begins its slow assent turning the blackness of night into a soft orange glow in the eastern horizon. Cactus and boulders come out of the shadows to be illuminated by nothing short of a breathtakingly beautiful Baja sunrise. Another energy drink down and whipping the dust and sweat from our eyes, we are still racing! Turning off the lights allows the drained electrical system a needed break. Two more checkpoints to go and we are right behind the truck we still need to pass for the win. Unfortunately, all they can do up to the final checkpoint is follow and eat the competitor's dust.

Now only 90 miles to go to the finish! There must be a place to finally pass the lead truck for the win. The trucks struggle it out. As spec trucks, they are built close to the same so neither has the advantage. It all comes down to skill and determination, and honestly some luck. Both trucks and driver crews have been pushed and beat to near limits with the finish line getting closer. The road opens to a dried lakebed. This is the chance to bump the speed high enough to finally make the pass. The competitor truck realizes this also and does not give up without a fight.

The driver instructs the co-driver to call the circumstances into the team anxiously waiting for news. The only way to beat this other truck is to push ours to the limit. We either win or blow the motor. A radio message comes back and says. "You are the one behind the wheel. Do what you need to do to win without killing yourselves." Time stops. Knuckles go white and they can feel their hearts beating in their chests. The motor is screaming into the redline. The GPS indicates 120 MPH. Slowly we pass the other truck with the throttled floored on a hope and a prayer we can keep it all together.

With an excited crackle over the radio, the co-driver announces that they have successfully passed the competitor and our truck is still holding it together. 40 miles to finish. Now 25. Now 10, and we are still in the lead. Five miles out with the hammer down and the competitor truck eating our dust. A small vibration is felt at first. Now becoming stronger and louder.

A circular rhythm that sounds like a flat tire? Front tires look good, must be one of the back tires and there are no more spares left abord the race truck. I call is made into the chase crews to find us near the finish line for a speed quick tire change. The team radios in that two other trucks in our class are directly behind us so there is not time to slow down now! The problem is the vibration has turned into a shredding tire now beating its way into the wheel well. Two miles to finish and one of our chase trucks is in sight requesting a location to change the tire.

The co-driver's voice comes alive over the radio, "One mile to the finish line, we can't stop or we will get passed. We are we coming in on three tires! Banks of lights illuminate a large group of spectators in the distance. We reach the finish line and roll up onto stage as the crowd cheers. High fives and shouts of excitement as the checkered flag drops!

Give Thanks
The next morning the dust has settled. Adrenaline has given way to exhaustion and everyone was able to get some much need rest. That afternoon we all meet at the local cantina for food and celebration. The experience and emotions of the last couple of days are hard to put into words. So much fun and excitement. So many adventures and experiences we will never forget. So many times when our team was pushed to the limits and people stepped to up to exceed expectations. So many lessons we have all learned on how we can do even better next time.

More importantly, so many reasons to give thanks:

> Thanks to all of those who have given so much to make this adventure possible.

> Thanks that no one got hurt.

> Thanks to the success we experienced as a team.

> Thanks for the opportunity to be able to have the privilege to participate in our favorite sport.

> Thanks for the friendships (old and new) and comradery of our team, our fans, others we have raced with, and those we met.

> Thanks to God who protected us every mile along the way.

Thanks to an exciting life and making memories with friends we will never forget.

With a click of glass cerveza bottles the team says, "Amen." "Cheers!" And, "Can't wait until next year!"

OK, admit it. Wasn't that fun?! Yes, it was, and think about how much more fun you will have pursuing your own dream. Don't wait, now is the time. Remember to keep the big picture in mind. That is what you are shooting for and what your race plan to get there? Remember that success comes in one small victory at a time as we conquer each leg of our life's journey.

The difference between winners and losers is that winners don't give up. No need to overthink each issue or problem. Winners get up, go, and do. No matter what happens they are still in the game, they keep racing! Win or lose, the honor goes to those with the courage to remain in the arena.

The Least You Need to Know

- Most missions are too complicated to ever do on your own requiring the need to create a team and work with others.

- You need to define your mission before you can sell it and recruit others to join and help you.

- Once someone buys into the mission, they can provide an amazing amount of effort, time, and money to help you see it through.

- Big missions are easier to tackle by focusing on *visually obtainable goals*. With the big picture in mind, get your team to focus on the current task so they can increase momentum by completing one goal at a time.

- Plans rarely go as intended. Use your leadership skills to foster communication, collaboration, and innovation to help take advantage of opportunities or solve problems fast.

- People are naturally competitive You as a leader need to convince them to collaborate and work together. Use their energy to compete against the competition instead of fighting with themselves.

- Praise your people in public, reprimand them privately.

- Team members can have different levels of contributes, some maybe owners with large, invested interests while others are part time volunteers. To win the race, the guy who found a spare alternator, and the other guy who installed it in the middle of the night is just as important as the owner and drivers of the truck.

- Win or lose, every experience has examples of things that were done right. Celebrate those. They also have examples of what can be learned from. Use those examples to make improvements to do even better next time.

- When your team works hard, give thanks, let them play and celebrate their success together. This builds rapport and increases effectiveness for taking on the next challenge together.

Chapter Eleven

Goldfish MBA

Know what you need to know until you capture the prize.
Shawn, Jeremy, and Javier find a Spanish chalice buried
in the Sacambaya Jungle, Bolivia, on Treasure Quest.

But wait there is more! Enjoy this bonus chapter at no additional cost. My goal has always been to go above and beyond and deliver more than what is expected. I have discovered these pearls of wisdom over the years that have served me well, so I am sharing them with you. This is practical, common-sense advice that coincides with the Goldfish Principles perfectly. They fit the theme and will save you and make you money while reducing heartache and wasted time.

Be Nice Until You Can't Be Nice
Said elegantly by Patrick Swayze in the movie *Roadhouse.* It is a good philosophy to live by. Your reaction should always be, act nice and be professional. Some could take your being nice as weakness. This is not the case as you also have to be assertive. Confident people do not overreact, yell, scream, and fight. They can smile and act professional in about any circumstance, even if they are raging mad on the inside.

I am not suggesting you be a doormat or give in to everyone else's demands. That is not acting nice, that is submissive. I am referring to the opposite of that which is assertive. Know what you believe and why, and stand your ground. Do the right thing and never let yourself be intimidated by others who want to use overly aggressive language or actions in the attempt to control you. Bullies will poke at you trying to get you to rage at them so they can become a victim to turn things around on you. Do not give them the satisfaction.

Like *Roadhouse*, bars have bouncers to keep the peace. They smile at you when you come in because they want your business. They keep an eye on you and are perfectly willing to pick you up and throw your ass to the curb if you become drunk and disorderly. They do this to protect the other patrons. Consider this in your own life, except it is to protect you and the ones you care about. If you must fight, legally or otherwise, document everything and be professional in everything you do or say. Even if that means picking them up and tossing them to the curb.

Cashflow is King

Garth and Sandy Brooks worked at a boot store in Nashville waiting for a record contract. The top actress or actor could be your table waiter in Los Angeles right now. No matter how much of a bigshot you are going to be, the rent is due now. Understand you must maintain positive cashflow, meaning you need to make more money than you spend. Be humble, suck it up, keep your job and don't quit until you can replace it with something better.

It's Cheaper to Buy What You Want the First Time

In my life, I like things neat and orderly. That means not being surrounded with extra junk and clutter. This helps me remain organized and keep my thoughts clear. I am saying this because it is easier and cheaper to ultimately buy what you really want once, than being a stuff collector. Maintaining things you don't use or need takes up precious time, money, and headspace.

For example, if you want a certain vehicle, house, job, or spouse, make a plan to get it. Many of us settle and get plan B or C, thinking we can always get what we really want later. This means buying the same thing over and over again, wasting time and money.

Making payments and maintaining something you really do not want and could be declining in value.

Getting what you really want will make you step up your game. You might have to be creative, even selling off the other cars and things you do not use. Getting what you really want should not mean burying yourself in debt. Don't do that either. It's like dragging a chain and will limit your options. Make a game out of it. First determine what you really want. Then ask yourself what improvements do you have to make in your education, career and self to obtain that? There is no bigger motivator.

Make getting what you want a reward for your hard work. For example, do not buy the car until you get the new job or client. Do not ask that dream date out until you have updated your clothing, and move into the new place. They will be impressed with the new you. Hussle and shine, extra money and opportunities will follow. Then you will save money and heartache by getting what you really want the first time.

Cookie Cutter Principle

A CPA friend once told me that he could look at about any business and determine if it will succeed or fail within minutes. Wow, this got my attention. "What is the secret?", I asked. He said the most successful and profitable companies make something once, mass produce it and sell it to the masses.

Think about it. Movies, books, software, music, fast food, etc. Not a lot of customizing. You make and sell something that most people want right out of the box. Even if you are in an industry with lots of customization, think about how you can use a cookie cutter to streamline your production.

Dance With the One Who Brought You

Being successful is about building and maintaining relationships. Someone took a chance on you, or they will before you were a hotshot. You need to honor the people who helped you, taught you, and gave you a job when someone else would not. There is always someone else offering you something shiny for less money or whatever, but do not sell out the people who invested in you first.

Discipline is the Difference

The theme of this book is there are not many shortcuts. You need to do the time and put in the work. How will you do this? Not by wasting time and binging on social media and TV. Many people are happy to always hit the easy button and do the absolutely least they can do and still get by. You are reading this book, that's not you. You have the desire for more in life, and you want it now. It will cost you, how are you going to do it?

Discipline. It means doing something even if you do not feel like it or have more fun doing something else. You will learn to embrace discipline because you know it is your ticket to success. You will not get what you want in life stoned and dreaming on the couch. The extra time and work you invest in yourself now will pay off big later for the rest of your life. What will you sacrifice to gain more later?

Get up a little earlier to get more done.

Learn to work when you do not feel like it.

Put time limits on meaningless activities and vices.

Reduce social media and binge-watching TV.

Learn to eliminate unhealthy relationships.

Block out time in your schedule to be highly productive.

Do not let others distract you or discourage you.

Almost everyone wants to lose weight or get in better shape. Buying a gym membership and getting the best-looking workout clothes will not do a thing. The ones who lose weight and get in shape are the ones who show up and sweat, working muscles until they ache. They do this because every time they do, they are that much closer to their goals. They can look in the mirror and see it. They do the work, even if they don't feel like, knowing it is worth it.

Do Not Let Anyone Define You

Do not let anyone define you! If I let my school counselor define me, I would be fixing your lawn mower right now. The action you take will define you more than anything else. Regardless of how humbling your beginnings are, you are the master of your own destiny. Action allows you to improve your circumstances and fulfil your life with meaningful progress.

What someone thought of you in the past is unimportant. The past is irrelevant as old news. When you are living your dreams, you have re-defined yourself! This allows you to define and shape the future you which is much more fun and productive than dwelling in the past.

Do Not Let Anyone Have Leverage on You
Live your life in a way that no one can honestly criticize you, blackmail you or hold you financially hostage. Do not acquire so much debt that you must stay in a job you do not want. Do not let anyone hold something over your head to control you.

Stay out of trouble, do your taxes, clean up your messes, save some money and do what you need to do to live with the ability to live under your terms, and reasonably worry-free. Maintain the flexibility to walk away from bad circumstances to take advantage of better opportunities.

Drop the Clock
Do not think about the day in the terms of nine to five. You should be 'on' after your first cup of coffee until you fall asleep. It does not mean you have to work every day, all day. But be aware that if you are constantly watching the clock or how many days until Friday, it is an indicator that you are bored or want to be somewhere else. And that is a strong indicator that you are doing something that you were not meant to do. When you are working and living your dream, doing what you are meant to do, you do not care what time or day it is. You are just happy to be in the game.

Drop the Victim B.S.
Some people are professional victims. They like the attention of always being the one who was done wrong. This thinking might provide some level of comfort when feeling sorry for yourself, but it is a dead-end way to live your life. Tough love time. You are probably not a victim. Some people are victims, something terrible happened to them they had no control over. Unlike the rest of us who are primarily victims of our own stupidity and years of bad choices.

Some of use are real victims having terrible, sometimes unspeakable things happen to them, and many find a way to power through and overcome. If they can do it, we can too. If your stupidity makes you a victim, you will have to use your new found purpose and common sense to work your way out of it.

Remember you are not entitled to anything and there are no free rides you will not have to pay for later. You get what you earn.
That is the way it should be and that is the way you want it to be. Achievement is what gives you satisfaction, confidence, and self-worth.

Enjoy the High-Tech Ride
With technology and the world changing so quickly, this is truly one of the most exciting times to be alive in history. You will have more opportunities than any other generation before you. I am old enough to have seen pixilated *Atari* TV video games to personal computers and the rise of the Internet. The advances over each decade will amaze us all. Electric cars to missions to Mars. Find a way to be part of it.

Everyone is a Volunteer
Yes, even you. That's why you must believe in your mission to complete it. You can be paid to show up, and you can pay others to show up, but you volunteer your heart to really be devoted to something. Treat others like volunteers. Not so much like you paid them to be there, but like they want to be there. It is important to focus on and sell the mission. What you are doing is so important, they want to be involved and are willing to volunteer their heart. This attitude helps create a team that will go the extra mile to get things done when you need them the most.

Find High Tide
Learn to understand your own mood tides. Think about it. The moon revolves around the earth, causing the ocean to tide high and low. As humans we also have our high and low mood tides throughout the day. Our mood can go up and down for no apparent reason. I am not going to blame the moon, but at some point of the day, maybe morning, mid-day, or evening, you feel your best. Maybe your good mood changes with no apparent pattern or schedule.

It's helpful to understand when you feel your best throughout the day. When down, that is your time to rest. When you experience high tide, and you feel the burst of energy, that is your time to be as productive as possible. Recognize when you are feeling good and ready to be productive. Even if it is only an hour, when you are up, you will be more productive, than hours of working during a low or natural high tide time.

Some people are lucky enough to schedule their best time for high productivity. Be aware of how you are feeling and use your high tide to your advantage.

Focus Like a Laser

As you become more successful, more people will depend on you to work your magic to make things happen. Your superpower with the rest of your abilities will determine your destiny. As your responsibilities grow, so will the distractions. Your increased success will make you a target for others that will want to relieve you of your money and time and provide every form of drama or distraction.

Be strong. When the pressure is on, these outside negative factors can only become stronger. Things will not always go well and you will feel the stress. You will be tempted to be distracted at best, or worse, fall into some addictive trap. Know your triggers and do not let it happen. Redirect your focus to the challenge at hand and remind yourself what success will feel like when you successfully complete it.

As the outside pressure increases, narrow your focus like a laser. This will allow you to use your innovation and creativity to burn through the distractions and drama. Disregard the temporary pleasure, it is worth it to enjoy true compete satisfaction of a job well done.

It Actually is Your Problem

It is fun to say, "Not my problem, not my monkeys, not my circus." This is a good attitude, because if it is not your problem, why engage the time, energy, money, and headspace to get involved in someone's mess? There is a 'but,' however. If it is something under your control and responsibility, it is your problem.

If it involves your family, close friends, career, or business, it probably is your problem. Using the ostrich technique of burying your head and hoping it goes away on its own never works. In fact, ignoring a problem only allows it to grow from something manageable to a much bigger mess. Take ownership, make others take ownership and take action to resolve molehills before they become mountains.

Legacy Building

A pastor friend once asked me about what my legacy will look like. Before he asked, I honestly had never thought too much about it.

He is right, we are only here for a short period of time, then our children will inherit our legacy whether it be good or bad. What do you want your friends, family, and acquaintances to think and say about you when you are gone?

Whatever they think or say is based upon your actions and behavior right now. In fact, everything we do, say and achieve builds our legacy. It is a good idea to zoom out to look at the big picture and what life could be like after we are gone. If we are not sure what action to take, ask, "What does it do for my legacy?"

Low Hanging Fruit is Rotten

There is no such thing as easy money. If it were really easy and paid well, all the low achievers that came before you would have snatched it up by now. Pyramid, multi-level marketing and criminal schemes, I have seen about all of them, and have not seen anyone who ever made any long-term money the easy way.

Your friends and family are gold. Never ever try to sell them anything or give their names up to a company so they can sell stuff to them. You will not make a living selling thing to your family and friends. They might buy something out of charity, but that is not the way you want to make money. It is not worth it, and you will only alienate yourself from the ones closest to you. If it is truly a good product there are ways to get it to market and sell to the masses. If you need to rely on grandma for a mercy sale, time to reconsider your career.

Low hanging fruit is rotten. You need to get a ladder and get to the top of the tree or a shovel and dig under the roots. Out of the mainstream, the least amount of people in an industry or the more specialized it is, that is where more money is earned. The only way to make easy money is to become good at your craft and become in high demand.

Money is Not as Important Than Knowing Who to Trust

That is a quote from the move *James Bond, Quantum of Solace*. When I was new at business, I was naive and trusted everyone. Honest people tend to think everyone else is too until you discover they are not. The first time you get lied to, cheated, or extorted, you are shocked.

Be around people long enough and it will happen. As you develop your career, you will soon discover who you want on your team and in your tribe and who you do not. Trust is more important than money and as Zig Ziglar once said, "You cannot do a good deal with a bad person,"

Monkey See Monkey Do

People are watching you, more than you can imagine. The bigger and more important you get, the more eyeballs will be following your every move. This includes your employees, co-workers, associates, the public, and your children. They are watching you to see what you do, what you say and how you handle yourself. They are wondering if they should do what you do.

You set the pace in your life and for others. If they see you show up late and goof off, they might too. If they see you carry yourself in a humane and professional way, you might just inspire them to do the same. If your world looks like a circus of wild monkeys, it could be because you are the ringleader. If you want to encourage, inspire, or influence the people around you, set the example and the pace. They are already watching you.

No Vampires

People can be defined by the energy they project. Some positive, some neutral, and some negative. Positive people leave you happy and encouraged. Neutral people can leave you bored, and negative people will make you feel as if they bit your neck and sucked the very life-blood out of your body. You feel drained, discouraged, and depressed. We can all think of examples of people we know in these categories.

The point is we want to spend as much time as possible with positive people. Neutral people in moderation and avoid negative people as much as possible. As you progress in your life and career, you will be asking much of your mind and body. You do not and will not have time to be down or distracted with someone else's drama. Find and hang with those who will be charge your batteries, not drain them.

One Year Later

A lady friend of mine is in an unhealthy relationship as she is with a man who is married. He promises he will divorce his wife to be with her, but it never happens.

Every year we have a discussion where she asks me what she should do. "He said this is the year he will finally divorce his wife to be with her." I remind her we had this same conversation last year and many years before that. I ask her what if we have this same conversation next year? Will you make the right choice then?

None of us are getting any younger and as we get older the years roll by faster. One year is a good time frame to evaluate your life. If there is something happening in your life you are not happy with and it has not changed over the last year, that is your green light to change it.

You gave it time to change and put it off, but it does not go away or resolve itself. Now is the time for you to be assertive to ensure your life changes for the best. Goldfish people do not waste time or let others waste their time. They take action every day to improve their lives. They know that ignoring a problem will not make it go away. It only makes it worse. Focus on what you want and get it, not what you do not want and settle for it.

Pick One Thing

Yes, I am a hypocrite, so I am asking you to do as I say not as I do. The most successful people pick one thing and become specialists in their field. They focus on a very specific specialty until they are known for their expertise in their industry. Unless in a small town, most doctors and lawyers do not just practice general medicine or law. The best discover a very small niche so they can distinguish themselves within that specialty. You cannot become too focused. Be very specific on what you will be good at and soar! This also helps others remember you. When others think about you or want to hire you, you want them to say, "Joe does ___ and he is the best at it." This is much more powerful than, "Joe does ___, ___, and ___, who knows what he is best at?" Be a specialist and be your best!

Pursue Excellence Not Perfection

Perfection is almost impossible, but excellence is achievable. I included this because many people do not pursue their dreams because they feel they are not perfect at them. Well, most people are not perfect, in fact, I would venture to say that no one or nothing is 'perfect.' With enough work, it can be excellent. It is good to pursue perfection, but ask yourself, is it excellent? Then ask, how do we make it even better?

Rock Stars are Rock Stars for a Reason

Admit it, you have dreamed about being a rock star. I think most have. And why not, they get to have all the attention and fun, making lots of money in the process. Rock stars might seem like goofy party animals that somehow got into the gravy train of fame, but it is not that simple.

Out of the many thousands of musicians and bands, rock stars worked harder than anyone else to make it big. While others gave up and took day jobs, rock stars kept working at their craft. They practiced for hours everyday for years. They wrote music, lyrics, and mastered their stage performance. Understanding they could not do it alone, they invested the time and energy to create a band of compatible people who could live, tour, get along and be business partners with each other.

That overnight success you see living their dreams has been working day and night for years. Here is something fun to consider. Every accomplishment you do is a song. A group of accomplishments over the last year or two is an album. Your self-image is the cover and your personal tag line is the title of the album. Would anyone buy it? Does it get radio airplay? You ready for prime time? Are you willing to do what it takes to be a rock star in your industry?

Say Yes to Yourself First

You have heard to pay yourself first before making financial obligations. I want you to think of your time like you do your money. As you become more important, sought after, and make more money, you will be pulled in even more directions with free time for yourself becoming a much rarer commodity. If you let everyone and everything else have their way with your schedule, there will be no time left for you, your family, or friends.

You need to block out time for you and your tribe. This is critical for your own well-being and for the relationships with your loved ones. For your own sanity, you need time for yourself to relax and do something you enjoy that does not include being bombarded with business related issues and phone calls. Saying yes to yourself means learning to say no to some other things that look like mission creep or are just not mission critical.

Understand Momentum

When political pundits analyze candidates, they look at polls. Polls, however, are a snapshot in time. More importantly is the candidate's momentum. Momentum is wind blowing for people and trends, and your life and career. You want to keep your productivity wheel spinning so momentum is on your side and moving in your direction. Momentum is created from your action. One small victory leads to the next, and the next, until your victories become big ones.

That is using leverage to pry and push until your achievements are complete. Then that latest achievement leverages your way into the next achievement. Your victories are used as a reason to connect with people who need to know what you have been doing. People who can hire you to pay you well for your skills and abilities.

Think of it this way - You are a large boulder on a hilltop. You have been sitting there for years, too big to move on your own. Then pry bars using leverage push on the bottom of the boulder. It's so heavy it does not budge. Then after relentless prying and pushing the boulder starts to move. Just a small movement at first, but then after more pushing and pressure, the rock begins to roll.

Slowly the heavy mass gives in and starts rolling. Since the boulder is on a hill, gravity now takes over and helps the rock roll faster and faster. Once this boulder begins its trip down the hill it is now unstoppable. Due to momentum, the rolling boulder is just too big and heavy to stop. It's now moving at full speed. Be the boulder and not anyone in its path! You are not happy because you win, you win because you are happy. That is confidence and momentum.

You Get What You Focus On

If you remember any of my nuggets of wisdom, remember this. If you focus on problems and drama, you get more problems and drama. If you focus on what you want to do, excellence and creating a great future for yourself, you can get that, too. Whatever you focus on is what you get more of. Where your mind goes, is where your actions and passions follow.

Most focus on what they do not want. The trick is to turn this around and focus on how you can achieve and obtain more of what you do want. This focus on the positive is one of the most powerful actions you can take.

It is so simple, yet so effective. I promise you, change your focus and attitude and you will improve your life for the better. Try it, what do you have to lose?

The Least You Need to Know

- Everything in the chapter. I promise you these lessons will all be relevant sometime in your life.

Chapter Twelve
Call to Action

A team celebrates a victory for getting their kayak from one island to the next in a leadership and teambuilding event in Puerta Rico.

You have been thinking and dreaming about your perfect life. I have too, but you know that thinking and dreaming are just the beginning. It is important to give your brain a visible path to follow and what the reward will look and feel like when you achieve it. Take the time to imagine how sweet your success will be. What you will do, who you will be with, where you will live, and how you will help others up along the way.

Then reality sets in. You know that no amount of dreaming, wishing, and hoping will change anything. It is about making a plan, rolling up your sleeves, and taking action. There are not many shortcuts other than what I have shared with you. No big secrets, gimmicks or schemes. Just you working smart, putting in the hours, managing resources, and leveraging one small victory into the next.

Enthusiasm and momentum grows as you become knowledgeable, experienced, and more sought after. More people will rely on your ability to work your magic to do the amazing and they will pay you more to do so.

Reality will set in again when you realize you are now living your dreams. Congratulations in advance. I promise you the satisfaction of doing so is worth it and it feels amazing. Hopefully I brought you to a happy place. Good, remember what it feels like. It is time to get to work!

7.   Build Your Brand

What can I do now?

_____
_____
_____
_____
_____
_____
_____

6.   Don't Fall into Traps

List activity I should avoid

_____
_____
_____
_____
_____
_____
_____

5.   Learn to Communicate

How can I become a better communicator?

_____
_____
_____
_____
_____
_____
_____

4. Educate Yourself

How will I learn more?

_____
_____
_____
_____
_____
_____
_____

3. What is your Superpower?

What am I good at?

_____
_____
_____
_____
_____
_____

2. Give Thanks

List who I can give thanks to

_____
_____
_____
_____
_____
_____

1.   Find your Mission

What do I want to do in my life based upon passion, what I'm good at, and profitability?

_____
_____
_____
_____
_____
_____
_____
_____

What can I do now to achieve my goals?

_____
_____
_____
_____
_____
_____
_____

What can you do over the next year to achieve my goals?

_____
_____
_____
_____
_____
_____
_____

What can you do over the next five years to achieve my goals?

_____
_____
_____
_____
_____
_____
_____

Jack's Goldfish Speech for 750 Boy Scouts

Jack's 2018 keynote speech for a Boy Scouts of America Rendezvous, Jasper, Oregon

QR Code Link to be scanned and played with a smart phone.

Youtube Link:
https://www.youtube.com/watch?v=Y8O_wu_6INU&t=195s

Index

134

A Heartfelt Thanks

I am a blessed man despite myself. A man of faults and imperfections, like you, no one is perfect. Or, maybe we are perfect? Beautiful crazy perfection just the way we are as we strive to do better and leave our mark on this world in a positive way. And lucky for us because God uses imperfect people to do this perfect work.

After all I have been through, both good and bad, I feel like I am just getting started. If I can do it, you can too. But I want you to bypass some of the mistakes and hardships and go right to the full throttle, high quality, full-life living. I want you to do just that. That's why I wrote the book. I pray that it will be a blessing to you.

I appreciate you buying *The Goldfish That Bared* and taking the time to read it. I know how many other options you have. That is why I included all the useful information I could think of to have the largest, most positive impact on your life as possible.

If you find this book helpful, please give it a review on *Amazon* and share it with someone else. If you have any feedback or if I could be available to be your group's next speaker, drop a line at: jack@donorthmedia.com Website is: www.donorthmedia.com

Thank you!

Jack W. Peters

"For I know the plans I have for you," declares the Lord, "plans to prosper you and not to harm you, plans to give you hope and a future." Jeremiah 29:11

Made in the USA
Middletown, DE
19 November 2020